SOUL RETRIEVAL:

RETURN TO WHOLENESS

SOUL RETRIEVAL:
RETURN TO WHOLENESS

Joanna Neff, M.A.

TRAFFORD
with *Light Expansion Publications*

The information in these pages is provided for educational purposes and is not intended to be a substitute for the professional medical diagnosis, advice or treatment obtained through a physician or other licensed health care provider.

Distributed by New Leaf Book Distributors in Lithia, Georgia, USA

Designed by Joanna Neff
Cover art, "Perception," and back cover miniature, "Spirited Son," by Teresa Dunwell, Louisville, CO 80027
Cover production assistance by Gregory Davis, Lafayette, CO 80026
Author photograph by Wendy Saunders, Lafayette, CO 80026
Word processed and copy edited by Joanna Neff

Canadian Cataloging-in-Publication Data

Neff, Joanna, 1948-
Soul retrieval: return to wholeness / by Joanna Neff
ISBN: 1-4120-1613-4
A cataloguing record for this book that includes the Dewey Classification and US Library of Congress numbers is available from the National Library of Canada. The complete cataloguing record can be obtained from the National Library's online database at: www.nlc-bnc.ca/amicus/index-e.html

TRAFFORD
PUBLISHING™
Offices in Canada, USA, Ireland and UK

Book sales for North America and international:
Trafford Publishing, 6E–2333 Government St.,
Victoria, BC V8T 4P4 CANADA
phone 250 383 6864 (toll-free 1 888 232 4444)
fax 250 383 6804; email to orders@trafford.com
Book sales in Europe:
Trafford Publishing (UK) Limited, 9 Park End Street, 2nd Floor
Oxford, UK OX1 1HH UNITED KINGDOM
phone 44 (0)1865 722 113 (local rate 0845 230 9601)
facsimile 44 (0)1865 722 868; info.uk@trafford.com
Order online at:
trafford.com/03-1990

10 9 8 7 6 5 4 3 2

To the late Risje S. Emming, my Dutch-American friend, whose support, love, and involvement in many early sessions helped form the foundation of this work .

CONTENTS

CONTENTS

CONTENTS

PREFACE

by Joanna Neff (Jyoti Alla-An [1]), Channel

There are two ways I could have organized this book: chronologically (by following my personal soul retrieval journey) or thematically (by following the flow of information essential to understanding the soul retrieval process in general). Having attempted both approaches, I can assure the reader that I have chosen the more coherent method—that what is provided here, sequentially, is the better way to help the reader understand why soul retrieval done *energetically* is so elegant, swift, and powerful.

Because this work, which I call "higher-dimensional soul retrieval" involves resolving karma from other lifetimes as well, I believe that it is critical to offer readers thorough discussions of such topics as Soul Groups and Reincarnation (as multi-dimensional expression). These subjects are explained both in the context of my work with Melora and directly through Melora, a

---

[1] I don't remember when I first realized that people can have spiritual names—meaning tonal descriptions of soul lineage. In the fall of 1987 (the first year of the six during which I lived in the mountains above Jamestown, Colorado, at about 8,700 feet), I was splitting firewood with a wedge and a sledge hammer. I asked out loud, of no one in particular: "What is my spiritual name?" As I was bringing the sledge hammer down, I heard: "Jyoti Alla-An." Years later, in a session with Melora and from the guide of another channel, I was told that "Alla-An" had to do with, respectively, a "starry" lineage and an angelic lineage. I had already known that "jyoti" in Sanscrit means "light."

guide who links me directly with my Higher Self during all sessions and at times when I'm going about my daily life.

Because my *personal* journey is illustrative of experiences others can share in going through their own soul growth, I believe it is also important to include information about this. Except for footnote text, much of this information can be found in Appendix sections, which include additional information about how the energetic approach to soul retrieval actually works, in process. I believe that including such information in the Appendices avoids intrusion on the flow of what continues to remain fascinating, and uniquely interwoven, material from Melora.

"Channeling"—from the Author's Perspective

Through Melora's energy I experience an instant knowing that the information is coming in on the light in the form of pure energy. Then it's re-translated. It's much as when you're talking into your phone and your voice goes through the fiber-optic strands as light. Then it comes out as sound again at the other end. But the voice is being translated into light, and light is the medium by which it travels. That's how I experience channeling. So, for me, channeling involves not only my own desire to ascend and to become whole but obviously also to discover my true Life Purpose. Because this involves teaching, communicating, and disseminating information, I can't really go too far into the "ozone."

For "Doubting Thomases"

(excerpts from a channeling workshop in Boulder, Colorado)

"The doubting Thomas part has more to do with the levels of people's belief that they can *communicate* with their Higher Selves, *merge* with them, channel them, or whatever term. WE understand that you don't really channel your Higher Self. We do understand that when you connect with your Higher Self you perceive a shift in energy; you perceive that you are channeling. However, in *conscious* channeling regarding your Higher Self you are not really channeling—you are merging in consciousness for that time.

Channeling your guides is a slightly different process. Your guides who are not in your 'soul hierarchy,' as our Jyoti puts it, are stepping forward, out of the Oneness, into individuation to communicate with you in a particularized form that you recognize as a being such as St. Germain[2] or your guide or guardian with a specific name. Therefore, the 'doubting Thomas' part is the ego part that is the first to be released in the process—as our Jyoti describes it—release to the *trust* now with your guides so that you may clearly channel what is actually coming through. You would then *not* reinterpret the information through your ego. Releasing fully to the guidance, you communicate the information that is intended—in the *form* that it is intended.

You will feel the resonance even with guides who may not be in your Soul Hierarchy because in working together you will feel more comfortable with their resonance than with the resonance of others. This is not a judgment of their character or of their value, lesser or greater, but simply an understanding that you are more comfortable with some than with others. (Why not be with those with whom you feel comfortable?)

Your guides will resonate similarly to you, as they resonate with your Higher Self, because all are working together in this merging of consciousness . . . and in *their own* soul growth. They are helping you develop, and you are helping them develop as well. So it's very much mutual work and not 'We are higher than you; you are lower than we'."

---

[2] Much research has revealed records documenting that St. Germain lived on the Earth for at least 300 consecutive years. One such book is *Count Saint Germain: The New Age Prophet Who Lives Forever*, by Arthur Crockett & Timothy Beckley. Included are interesting accounts that St. Germain was "one of the selected representatives of the French Masons at their great convention in Paris in 1785" and that St. Germain visited Mesmer (father of hypnosis through his theories of "animal magnetism") in 1889 or 1890. What resounds is people's amazement that St. Germain never seemed to age.

Melora's Agenda

"In giving this information to you, it has been our intention to explain how an entire group can ascend. For this to happen, we make suggestions about what is the most opportune, at this 'time,' for all. There are portals of maximized opportunities for all in a soul group, and this is one of them—what you have termed this new millennium and the ten years or so after that. The sense of urgency is to take advantage of the acceleration that's possible in this optimal time. We take advantage of this opportunity by amplifying conscious awareness of the multi-dimensional selves through our connection with Jyoti, as an example—facilitating it, intensifying it, clarifying it, raising it vibrationally so that her energetic field becomes elevated more and more, as we are also doing at our 'levels'—all of us as a group. This group may be considered all the 'selves' of Jyoti Alla-An. " — Melora

Melora has many times said that "Ascension is expansion of consciousness"—that where you focus is where you are in consciousness. Two aspects of Melora's perspective on ascension distinguish her work. One is that Ascension[3] is ongoing; it is an evolutionary process. The other is that in order truly to understand this process we must include all our other "lifetimes" (including future lives), not just this current lifetime. Melora says that although one may ascend from this one lifetime, this does not mean that the hosts of other co-existing lifetime expressions of a person will also have ascended.

Indeed, Melora states that to ascend it is important to understand this interdependency of consciousness among incarnational expressions. In order to ascend from this current lifetime, it is critical to retrieve lost soul aspects (or soul fragments). By the same token, in order to to ascend it is necessary to merge in con-

---

[3] Ascension is expansion of consciousness beyond 3rd-dimensional consciousness. Many of "New Age" beliefs aspire to do this while still in the body. In order to reach "Christ Consciousness," one must attain at least 5th-dimensional consciousness, which is the vibration of total Love.

sciousness with other incarnational expressions, who are like soul fragments to one's Higher Self.

This emphasis on soul retrieval and multi-incarnational merging is the foundation of the work that Melora and I now do together to help people complete their ascension work. Soul retrieval as performed by Melora and other higher-dimensional beings is done energetically through their bringing the "fragments" and the core soul into harmonic resonance by recalibrating the signature energies.

Because, as a guide, Melora links me directly with my Higher Self, this work we do together benefits all in what I call "my vertical soul hierarchy." During my many years of association with Melora, it has been clear that SHE continues to learn and grow through ME! Her flexibility, her unconditional love, her compassion—all these have taught me much about relationship with the Divine. It has taught me how critical our consciousness within incarnation is to the spiritual development of non-physical versions of ourselves in higher dimensions. Most importantly, working with Melora has taught me about how honored we are by all the higher beings in the light, who fully appreciate the difficulty of being light workers in 3rd Dimension.

Expertise I developed during my initial two years of channeling laid the groundwork for my current work with Melora in higher-dimensional soul retrieval. With the help of an adept channel and her guide, I learned to clear and protect myself, channel accurately—without Ego interference—and to discern those discarnate spirits who merely wanted to "step up to the microphone" after I opened to channel. In these taped sessions, both the other channel and I received much healing, including the kind of higher-dimensional soul retrieval I facilitate for clients today.

I channeled much of the core content of this book during the first two years of my "apprenticeship" as a channel. My publishing a new age tabloid called *The Light Expansion "Times"* (L.E.T.) allowed exposure to the subject matter at a time before I had any idea of creating web pages to publicize the work I do with Melora.

PREFACE

It still amazes me how coherently interwoven are three of the articles I published originally in *L.E.T.* The first, about soul retrieval, was published in February, 1994; the second, about soul groups, was published in February, 1995; the third, about reincarnation (Melora's point of view) was published in November, 1995. Eventually, I would re-edit and publish these articles in *The Sedona Journal of Emergence*. The *Sedona Journal* presented "Soul Retrieval: The Return to Harmonic Resonance" (September 1997), "Reincarnation As Multi-dimensional Expression" (November 1997), and "Soul Groups: Your Soul Niche" (February 1998).

More importantly, this early work continues to reflect the path of my own spiritual development, because, as Melora has said: "Consciousness is ALL. What you are not conscious of is virtually useless to you." Because I am a conscious channel, information that comes through me also registers in my consciousness and helps me continue to grow.

INTRODUCTION

What Is Soul "Fragmenting"?

During profound stress, pain or other trauma, human beings often experience what is called "soul loss"—meaning, the loss of aspects of one's soul. Such events as loss of a loved one, automobile accident, surgery, addiction, combat trauma, abortion or miscarriage, and physical abuse are the prime causes.

When a soul is fragmented one may no longer remember the details of the traumatic incidents that caused the fragmentation. The "lost" soul aspect has taken those memories with it. When a soul part leaves, it may also take with it a measure of one's vitality. The more severe the trauma, the more life force is depleted.

As a result of this reduced life force, people who have lost soul aspects may suffer chronic illnesses in childhood. One example of soul fragmenting occurs because of childhood sexual abuse. Here, parts of the soul literally leave because the event is too painful. If the soul fragmentation is severe enough, such illnesses as schizophrenia may occur. Because the integrity of the parts to the whole is broken down, recovery is seen as an impossibility. Further, the will may become vulnerable to negative entity attachment.

Having fragments remain "unincorporated" between lifetimes affects karma because issues encapsulated in the consciousness of those fragments remain unresolved. In addition, if we remain unconscious of our other multi-incarnational lives, we bring them with us to our "next" incarnation, hopefully to awaken us to the reality that they're "out there."

After Soul Retrieval

Upon the return of lost soul aspects most clients feel a sense of well-being and wholeness. Often there is a return of childlike joy, exuberance and vitality. For many there is also a dramatic shift in consciousness—a sense of personal power balanced in a new level of heart/spirit connection. After soul retrieval, abilities and talents that previously were inhibited (or blocked) begin to be expressed fully once more.

During Soul Retrieval

(excerpts from a private session)

MELORA: During a soul retrieval session, the reality of experience of the Soul aspect as it leaves is brought back to you to experience for a short time. This is a question that our Jyoti had too, because she suddenly got a sore throat, and there was something about how every time she swims in that blankety-blank indoor pool she gets an ear infection. Well, this is a sort of auto-drowning and chronic strep throat—and as a baby her ear infections, and so on.

She rightly guessed today that the reason . . . she sort of cursed herself because she no longer believes in manifesting these illnesses anymore. But the soul fragment that brought this back doesn't know the difference. So she guessed correctly that these symptoms really manifested as a strong energetic remembrance of a soul aspect not quite adjusted yet to the current belief structures.

It's important in the process of soul aspect integration to determine that this is indeed going on and to understand in your belief structures that it's not necessary for it to go on for long. You don't need to *keep* it manifested. Talk to that soul aspect and tell it, "I understand that this is you, and this is your experience. We have a new way of being now. Welcome home! But we don't have to do this anymore." This would speed up the integration process.

Another aspect is that in the body's healing processes, when you make an adjustment in one place, then there may be a place temporarily out of adjustment somewhere else, until it's totally aligned. If your neck is getting adjusted somewhere, then your head may—or, say, in the skull structure there may temporarily be pressure or pain. We work to fine-tune and align in these ways.

QUESTION: Is this because of integrating the fragments, or is it the spirit guides working?

MELORA: Both. The memory in the tissues that the soul fragment brings back to you is an actual sensation, because this was the experience of the soul aspect in its last in-body experience that it took with it. As it comes back in, you will feel a transient *vivification*, if you will, of whatever it was that this aspect experienced exactly at the moment of leaving—or what state, what perceptions of your reality.

The intent is most important. There are ways of working with energy that vary according to the unique gifts of individuals, in bodies and not in bodies. There's a sort of personality thing involved too. We, as you, vary in our abilities to, as you say, visualize, or be sentient—which all means how one uses energy. We have our preferred ways of using energy.

Some like to be very dramatic and flamboyant. The shamanic soul retrieval is, in a way, a dramatization that allows people to have a sense of journeying, bartering, trying to coax—things that make sense in the human domain. In going through these processes one is really just clarifying for oneself each successive step. It's a way slowly to alter the belief structures to accommodate the aspects' coming back.

There are ways to do this in a purely energetic fashion, which we have done with Jyoti since she had human help to do this. She needed her belief structures to change so that the rest could be done energetically. It was her free will and her desire to do it in this fashion. She opted not to go the shamanic route. Although she felt that the story-line approach and the journeying were symbolic and very beautiful, she didn't need them in order to believe that the process was going on. Some people do, however.

The Author's Initial Soul Retrieval Work

Melora has stated that entire "past lives" must be retrieved as fragments. After my initial work with Mary H. on October 10, 1994, in channeling sessions I worked with my personal guides and St. Germain to finish my own soul retrieval. Because I was channeling, I was able to tape record the "play-by-play" going on with my guides.

My guides and St. Germain worked with me in four sessions, during which they also did some intensive healing of my physical body. They worked with restoring my etheric template (one's perfect physical blueprint). They retrieved two major past lives as fragments. I had glimpsed these lives in two separate past-life regressions—one in 1979 and one in 1985. I remember that at the beginning of each hypnotic regression I was told that the lives I would see would be appropriate to the lessons of *this* life.

Actually having entire past lives brought back during soul retrieval tied up some loose ends for me. My guides retrieved a soul fragment/past life from 1700s France—a life I had re-experienced in a 1979 hypnotic regression in Athens, Ohio, with Sharry Edwards. Sharry is now doing phenomenal healing work with bioacoustics.[4] Thus, apparently at a time when Sharry was just getting started in her work, I had the chance to work with someone who's now rather famous in her field. I certainly wasn't a "New Age" person in 1979. I just always have been inquisitive.

---

[4] Bioacoustics is a trademark of Sharry Edwards, M.Ed., of the Sound Health Research Institute in Albany, Ohio. *Merriam-Webster* defines *bioacoustics* as: "a branch of science concerned with the production of sound by and its effects on living systems." This term, as applied to humans, now refers specifically to the research initiated by Sharry Edwards in the 1970s, of voice spectral analysis and the presentation of sound frequency to support normal form and function.

In this session with Sharry I remembered that my name in this 18th Century past life in France was Angela, that apparently I had been orphaned, and that I had become the ward of some kindly elderly gentleman. I had every material advantage one could want, and yet I was unhappy. In the session, Sharry had me go to the Hall of Records, where a small book materialized in my hand. It was a diary, and although I could see the configuration of the handwriting in French, I was unable to read it—except for the date: 1736. (I somehow *got* that I was 13 years old at the time I was reading the book.) However, as I gazed at the book I burst into tears, realizing it had been my mother's diary. Many years later, working with the guide of another channel in Boulder, Colorado, I was able to remember more-specific details of this past life.[5]

Having my guides retrieve two separate past lives made me realize that there have been links in consciousness in my own life—as far out of touch and as spiritually unaware as I thought I had been in the past. Through this work I see that, all along, I've been moving in this direction. It wasn't something that just "happened" to me out of the blue. I don't just happen to live in Boulder, Colorado. I saw my own soul's yearning to come back to this Oneness, and I know that back, so many years ago, there was this link to the process I continue to experience with my guides.

---

[5] For more information about this, and other, of the author's past lives, see Appendix C.

CHAPTER ONE:

Shamanic Soul Retrieval

Animal Totems & Archetypes

(excerpts from a private session)

Animal totems that you may experience as medicine animals through shamanic means are not actually there. This is the mechanism of communication from your Higher Self to you about what's going on with you. In other words, the animals are not *literally* there. They are symbols, but the energy is, literally, information. The medicine animals are symbols of information coming through in the form of precise energies, and the symbols are coming through so that you can identify those archetypal resonances that each represents.

When you experience visions about interaction with, or literally *being*, such animals, you are being given information about *you* from your Higher Self. All symbols as they've come through "mythology" have served this purpose. The archetypes of everything that you can choose to be exist in the coding of your DNA. And so what you're familiar with in your *milieu* here on Earth is what you're going to attach those possibilities or archetypes to, including archetypal medicine animals or power animals. Also: certain roles that you play—villain, predator or victim, and so on.

Specific qualities that you ascribe to certain animals make you fearful. Some of them are predators and some of them are not; some of them swim the ocean and some do not; some of them use sonar and so forth. These are the specific identifiable aspects of all possible archetypes with which you resonate. Your personal power animals, your shamanic remembrances, and so forth, are all going to be about *you*. They're going to be information about who you are in all your multi-dimensional expressions, but the images are coming as Earth images. Do you see?

When we do soul retrieval we are energetically triggering these very archetypes that are in your DNA. The same energetic structures that represent these archetypes are what are encoded in certain power crystals. You're getting triggered, and so if you're going to be getting shamanic images and medicine animal images, then obviously your particular way of interpreting these has to fall within that classification—medicine animals—although it could be something totally different. It could just be conceptual. It might be in Greek. However, for you what resonates are very ancient Aztec, Amerindian, shamanic associations, and so your answers, here, with these are always going to be within that context of interpretation.

That does not mean that they're restricted to this; this is just the way the information is coming to *you* because of the intensity of your remembrance of incarnate experiences. That's what they have in common: that shamanic, animal-magic kind of archetype.

Thus, your answers are going to be for your earthly mind, and your consciousness, at this point, and you'll find answers in such books such as *Animal Speak*[6] that include very exotic animals—not just the basic ones. What does the book say about the cougar, about the jaguar? There you will find your answers, but all of it is about you. A network (or strands) of energy connects your Core Soul with all its lost soul aspects, and this connection is what draws them in during soul retrieval.

(from a group channeling in Boulder, Colorado)

QUESTION: I've got a question about crystals. They've got spirits of animals in them. I've read that an entity will choose to inhabit a particular crystal and trade this as an image, as a bridging for anyone who sees it to connect to that entity. Is that true as you see it? And, if so, how is it done and what level of being are these that come through this way?

MELORA: We wish to describe it this way, and we will talk of shamanic journeying again: The power animals, as they're termed (your "animal guides" as they're termed as well), are energetic representations of what enlivens that animal—what specific quality of energy you associate with that animal. So in a way it's like an exalted energetic version of that animal. This is why, in a shamanic journey, the animal guide has so much power and why you relate its energy in a more subtle way to the feline in your house. You see, you're working with the black jaguar, and that resonates with your cat, but this is even more intense.

As with shamanic work, *you* are directing the use of those energies. In that way, the consciousness in the crystal is said to be passive. If the consciousness within the crystal is *directed*, then that is a different matter. You see, the encoding in crystals is essentially passive. Because of the latticework structure and the free ex-

---

6 *Animal Speak: The Spiritual & Magical Powers of Creatures Great & Small*, by Ted Andrews. Llewellyn Publications, 1993. 383 pages.

change of ions on the surface back and forth, because it can replicate itself, store information and use that information in its environment, it is truly like DNA.[7]

However, you, as the person with the crystal, are directing what could be considered as the energy archetype it contains, whether you interpret that as an animal essence, a consciousness like a Lemurian consciousness, or a starseed crystal like this is [referring to Jyoti's "Melora crystal"]. This is like "ET, phone home." This is a starseed crystal right to our Jyoti's source.

The mechanism is passive—"bridging," as you actually said. When you perceive devic energies and consciousness in crystals as they are housed in them, it is more of an impression in the crystalline matrix than it is an *actual* consciousness, directing itself out of the crystal. Is this understandable?

QUESTION: Yes. It's more of a cue to a certain kind of energy?

MELORA: A "computer" *program*. A holographic computer program.

QUESTION: Similar to . . . I have a cross. It has archetypal energies that you have identified it with, that you can access as a cue to keep yourself focused . . .

MELORA: That is how you *use* it, but the archetypal energy actually exists without your recognizing it. That's correct. Thank you for your question. We love questions on energies!

Symbolism and Shamanic Soul Retrieval

(excerpts from a private session)

SW: In one of our last sessions, we were working with the wheel of my different spirit helpers. I remember there was the dolphin and

---

[7] *Windows of Light: Quartz Crystals and Self-Transformation*, by Randall N. and Vicky V. Baer. Harper & Row, 1984. 176 pages.

other members within that wheel. This is what I'm getting down to: The disembodiment of me and the putting me back together. When I completed the wheel—which meant there were 12 animal spirits—at 11 o'clock there was a cougar. Everybody attacked me and tore me apart (and a cobra was part of the wheel). Two cobras came in, and as I observed, they spun back around like DNA, in a double-helix, and put me back together again.

I was working with a shaman earlier this year. In his book he talks about the disembodiment and the observing that goes on. I wanted to ask you about that and thank you for setting me on that path, as I recall, to get the 12 and to see what would happen. The shaman I worked with also said that it is possible to have more than one of these disembodiments.

MELORA: Something we observed with a friend of our Jyoti's will explain how we view such shamanic processes. When this friend received higher-level Reiki[8] attunements from Jyoti and another mutual friend, her experience was that the Hindu goddess Durga came in and tore her to shreds, chopped her head off, and all this sort of thing. People who do not do shamanic work do not experience these *translations* of energetic processes in the same way.

In shamanic work, as we have said, there's a lot of symbology. But shamanic work also works with archetypes. These archetypes would be of all human experiences, all possible roles—like specific villain/good guy, predator/victim—all the possible roles that you could choose on earth to be and that you *are* throughout history in your many lives. We're receiving that your interpretations, your

---

[8] Reiki is a very ancient, spiritually guided life force energy that is said to have been used by Gautama Buddha for healing. Rediscovered in the mid-1800s, Reiki is literally able to perform healing miracles. It can actually be seen by clairvoyants, and the Reiki "beam" of high-vibrational light has been captured in Kirlian photographs. Reiki not only reduces pain and stress but also has a profoundly positive effect on health problems, minor and serious. Reiki works on all levels: physical, emotional, mental and spiritual.

experiences, your visions are translations of the energies into symbologies that represent archetypal experience.

We believe we told you before that these are *not* to be taken literally. The danger in taking these literally is that you confuse the *translation* with the actual processes that are going on. There can be distortion. This creates fear, because if you take the symbols of being torn apart literally, and that creates fear, then the processes remain incomplete, and you can't move forward into the integration of what happened. *Such confusion between symbology and actual energetic processes are the basis of superstitions!* And superstitions are almost always fear based.

SW: Okay. I thought of it as more of a rebirth or a restructuring— that the witness part of me stepped out of that and didn't find it humorous, but at the time it was a sort of shock because they all just sort of attacked me.

MELORA: Because shamanic work generally goes no higher than 4th dimension, or the astral plane—

SW: Oh. I didn't know that.

MELORA: With shamanism the work is primarily physical and psychological. Thus, the restructuring is really going on in your psychological consciousness—that is, personality consciousness— not at the Soul level. This is why we find that, for example, certain people come to us for higher-dimensional soul retrieval after shamans have done soul retrieval because these particular people are rife with negative entities. *It's not that the work itself created that; it is that the result of incomplete processing of psychological changes and structures leaves the person vulnerable to astral-plane influences.* This is where the negative entities "hang out": in the lower octave of the astral plane. If people are not strong enough in their mastery or in their wisdom, then they are not really able to participate out of that wisdom, or out of a higher consciousness, in the work that is being done by the shaman.

SW: Can you check me to see how I fit in to the scenario that you just described?

MELORA: Give us a moment. Yes. What we're hearing is that the abilities you have, not only from past lives but also from this life and the interest that you have in shamanic work, are like traps in a way. You can keep using the skills that you already have, or you can learn some new skills. What they're saying is "spiritual skills." Can you transcend your intense personality interest at these levels, and move to manifesting at higher levels and move to processing at higher-dimensional levels?

SW: I'd like to be able to do that, but I think I might need some help or guidance.

MELORA: All right. We will do this in the way of a parable to help you use some more multi-dimensional understanding of this. One of the last temptations of Buddha was having a demon come to him and try to engage him in an intellectual debate. In other words, "Let's talk and we'll find out who's more brilliant." **At the personality level, what your mind affixes on that is interesting to it can actually be a great temptation that keeps you from coming to higher spiritual consciousness.**

SW: It's also a very beautiful trap.

MELORA: They are very beautiful traps, because the mental gymnastics appease and entertain the mind. The problem is that you keep having to do more of it, because if that is what your mind is used to being fed, then it's like an addiction. It has to keep going on and on; it has to keep being fed. *If you're can come out of the personality mind's need to have information for its own sake to entertain it, then you can transcend the personality level of consciousness that is in to confusing symbology with reality.*
Confusing symbology with reality is a trap. You can take the same information and process it in the same way we have described—the intense emotions of grief, loss that you're going

through now—and ask for that to be distributed among <u>all</u> your bodies and processed so that you get the real *experiential values* these represent. Make the request of your guides, your Higher Self and your Overbeing to make that clear of you. Then you will come to a center of wisdom in which fear will go away. You will have great clarity and understanding that **symbols *do not exist at higher levels***. They exist only in 3rd and 4th Dimension.

SW: How interesting, because a lot of the teachers I've been with in this embodiment have stressed the importance of the symbol.

MELORA: But why is it important? Is it important to you spiritually or to you as a being in 3rd-dimensional existence?

SW: I think a lot of the reason is that it's a power source—a power *over* instead of power itself.

MELORA: Yes. Exactly.

SW: I know that for some people the information became power *over* and not power itself, and I was trying to keep away from that, even at that time. That goes back probably ten years. Thank you. It's kind of nice to hear that come back to me. It's almost like a confirmation of something hidden very deep inside.

MELORA: Exerting power over others is always of the dark, although, yes, this can be a matter of degree. There can be "relative" darkness, if you will. We're not saying that all shamans who do that, or all white Wiccans who do that, are of the dark. What we're saying is that **you're missing the point spiritually in your existence on Earth if you don't realize that power over others is always about fear**. And since fear is the opposite of love, it's going to take you in the opposite direction of your path to the light, which is the path of Love. It can take you away from your Self, as you so perceptively put it.

SW: I had felt that to be true and have not been fighting against it but have not quite understood why so many people are so interested in the *power-over* aspects, which again represents fear.

MELORA: Everything that comes forth in a session is always aimed at your initial, question, the central *motif*, that compelled you to have a session. So it is not just a conversation; it is about the deep question you had in coming to work with us today.

SW: One of the other questions I had was about what happened during our last session when my wife and I met on the rainbow bridge. I revisited that, and although she didn't come to the middle of the bridge, Pegasus came over and there was also a wolf—a very beautiful wolf that she connects with. The wolf actually came to the middle of the bridge, lay down and exposed her underbelly. I played with the wolf, and it felt very good until Pegasus and my wife started to come onto the bridge. I got the feeling that she was a little reluctant to do this. In fact, she may even have gone back to *her* side [of the bridge]. I wanted to thank you for giving me that process and my ability to revisit that on a journey. It was very beneficial to me to have both the wolf and Pegasus.

MELORA: Yes. Because **it's about true spiritual power, which is in receiving—not doing**. It's in being-ness. If you think about all you've heard and read about where it is desirable to go in the Ascension process, it is into pure being-ness. If you allow yourself to experience that here, if you will, in 3rd dimension, that is the answer to your question. We have come full circle in this session. That is the answer to your question about how you "get there." The goddess energy is key in getting to that next level.

Shamanic power is very *yang*, very male, very 3rd- and 4th-dimensional. Goddess energy—moving into the love vibration—is a much more *yin*, female kind of receptivity to allowing *descension*, to allowing the ascension of consciousness, just allowing the merging, which is symbolically characterized by this vision of your wife. Allowing merging. Therefore, your whole Ascension process is symbolized here.

SW: Well, that answers the question about the 30 years and why we're still together I guess.

MELORA: Yes, you still have this work to do, and it is critical in moving you into the space you say you wish to be. As you allow that here, in the relationship with your wife, so then do you pave the way and open the door to moving into that other consciousness of spiritual ascension.

CHAPTER TWO:

Reincarnation as Multi-Dimensional Expression

Melora discusses "reincarnation" from her vantage point as a group consciousness. As usual, her perceptions are not only unique but also "ring true" for those who are open to hearing about what reincarnation really means in our current experience. She emphasizes the importance of coming to consciousness of our multi-dimensional existences so that we may accelerate our ascension process.

It is possible to ascend after the releasing of the body from the 3rd-dimensional existence As we have explained, **what you call reincarnational lives are really simultaneous lives. Each of these other 3rd-dimensional lives is affecting your growth in this life, and *vice-versa*. It has been suggested in the various books on this subject, truly, that in order to ascend you *must* (and this is**

one of the few times that we use this strong language of "must") become conscious of these other lives.

What is holding many people back is that they are still immersed in the illusions of 3rd-dimensional reality in <u>all</u> of their simultaneous lives. If in just one lifetime expression the consciousness expands to a certain point, the consciousness of the One (which some have termed "Christ consciousness"), this opens up the same possibility for the other multi-dimensional lives. You are a seed self of your Higher Self. Each of your other lives in 3rd Dimension is a seed self of your Higher Self. So as each of these multi-dimensional lives achieves the consciousness of that Higher Self (meaning your Core Soul Self, your Exalted Self), then it is possible to become conscious of the next level, which we have termed the Oversoul. This is apart from your conception of dimensions. These are all expressions of the same Self, and this is the microcosm that the First Set represents: the relationship of Source Creator to all its creations.

About "Historic" Lives

The human mind in 3rd Dimension often questions how there can be entire, apparently linear, "histories" that you can study, like the Middle Ages, the Renaissance, the Victorian Era. Why is it that simultaneous existences seem to be linear? If they are simultaneous, then how can you read in a history book that this age occurred first and that age occurred next? In the rules of 3rd-dimensional reality there is TIME, and there is the restriction of 3rd-dimensional understanding. In order to make that play out for you as convincingly as it does, there need to be some "bleed-throughs" of other multi-dimensional existences. For the most part, you receive only those of the "past," because your belief structures have not so readily accepted that you can access "future" events the way you access "past" events.

Of course, from our perspective there is no difference. It is all fluidly in the NOW. In the rules where your consciousness is focused, however, it is necessary for there to be a bleed-through in a linear fashion so that you have some sense of time passing—some sense of a "chronological" history, so that you can experience a relationship of the past in a progression. This progression is designed to *seem* to be chronological and developmental, or else these rules would simply disappear and you would not have the structure that you need in order to learn the life lessons that all have incarnated here to learn. Thus, your reality is a sort of holographic creation, a sort of psychodrama, if you will, with this rule of time. If you did not have a sense of starting somewhere and progressing and coming here, then it would not work in this way.

The Pleiadians said (in *Bringers of the Dawn*[9]) that you must become conscious of your multi-dimensional selves. This is true. However, this does not have to be a total awareness. If you understand that, say, in a past life in the moment before death when there is the common experience of going toward the light and understanding the Oneness—that moment of awareness links all of your multi-dimensional selves together in consciousness. This particular state of enhanced being in which you find yourselves as you have begun this new millennium is much like having the "veils" taken away. The curtains part, and you literally see: "Oh! There I was in such-and-such a life." Then those lives become conscious of each other. In the instant of such a consciousness connection what you are really doing is coming into oneness with those selves, and if you have only a glimpse of those past lives and they of you, then what the Pleiadians noted is accomplished.

By the way, we do energetically perceive the difficulty of understanding this with the 3rd-dimensional brain because in trying to explain it clearly we have experienced great difficulty. Reincarnational relationships are complex in many ways and simple in many ways. Picture yourself in that life standing on the left. Say, this is your life in Afghanistan as a woman who has to wear veils from head to toe. There is a sense of restriction being expressed here—and inequality. We will say that these are the issues, hypothetically, so we'll have the Afghanistan experience be in the "past" (not parallel in time), just so it's not too mind-boggling.

---

[9] *Bringers of the Dawn: Teachings from the Pleiadians*, by Barbara Marciniak with Tera L. Thomas. Bear & Company, 1992. 288 pages.

Now picture the Higher Self just "above" this as part of what will be a triangular kind of form. Thus, in the Afghanistan life you are suffering and feeling totally disempowered, and the Higher Self, of course, is in constant communication—at least from the "location" of the Higher Self. We're now drawing a line "up" from the Afghani woman to the Higher Self, and this woman is bemoaning her experience. As the Higher Self we "get" this.

Now see the other side of a triangle coming "down" to the expression of you, "now," on the right, over here. In that way you're connected here at the base of the triangle, energetically, because through the Higher Self you are getting what is termed as a "bleed-through" from another life. The bleed-through is made possible because of the resonance to the Higher Self back-and-forth, not between the incarnations "sideways."

The intention is that with the increasing intensity of this "beam" relating to the issue(s), hopefully one of your incarnate expressions is going to get it. That is, you go into your higher mind, your higher emotion, your Higher Self, and you focus there. Not only do you get relief from your illusion of suffering but you also grow spiritually as a result of going to a higher level of consciousness in experiencing a Oneness instead of feeling imprisoned, incarcerated, unequal and disempowered.

Jyoti was thinking that the connection was more "lateral," meaning that, for example, she would go "sideways," if you will, to her Elizabethan life in a direct line through the DNA. This is not how it happens. The connection is through the Higher Self—as the Higher Self is able to "break through" in consciousness to each individual life, then through the elevated consciousness of each of the expressions back through us, through the next one and back to us, and to the next one and back to us (center-out-across) with the Higher Self as a sort of Grand Central Station.

Multi-Dimensional Selves

There is an infinite number of possible selves. Take *our* "group" as an example: It is just the group of one Oversoul, Higher Self, all the multi-dimensional seed selves (past, present and future in

36

your terms), the fragmented soul aspects, the possible selves, and so on. This is ongoing. With the usual interpretation, the suggestion always seems to be that there is a sort of finite point at which these things end and that you can then count them all and say, "There are this many, and this is when they ascend." This is all going on simultaneously at a level of infinity impossible even for us to fully "understand" in our consciousness. If we could, we would not be "merely" where we are now, if you understand.

We shall attempt to explain. Each multi-dimensional self has a separate consciousness—individuated out of the One, as St. Germain is, or as we are when we come to you. All are "tied together" in consciousness. We are an individuated being, a manifestation that "steps out," if you will, of the consciousness of the One and expresses itself as a "personality" so that, on this plane, people will recognize us (and because of your need to ask, "Who are you? What is your name? What message do you bring?") This is an individuated consciousness as an expression of the One, as one of the infinitude of expressions of the One that you call this Universe, all of the inhabitants of it and all of the stars and planets in it—all of the creations that express it.

Thus, it is not just you who are ascending from this life, at this time, on this Earth. Soul groups, as a whole, go through the ascension process together. If you remember that the process of what you term ascension is ongoing—and that it always has been and that it always will be—it will seem more like moving up and up and up in "rows."

If you would picture an Oversoul that at one time was one incarnational expression of the Higher Self—then you will see that in the so-called process of ascending from one level to the next, and to the next, and to the next, there is a direct connection "linearly" from Oversoul, to Higher Self, to once-incarnate expression. Now, the creative relationship is that when Spirit allows a certain consciousness it is able to create extensions of itself, spiritually—to come into incarnation (as a main example), although we do create other kinds of possible selves that you might interpret as "future" or alternate selves, meaning that we might also be ex-

pressed as a nature elemental or as an angel. If you see us as crea-
tors or co-creators, these would still be individuated in their expression. Because these creations have the same source, even
though they have what are apparently different expressions, they
are connected energetically through the Higher Self.

As your consciousness develops, when you access your Higher
Self you are also given access to your other multi-dimensional
expressions. Since this doesn't go across laterally, it's not as
though you can resonate "sideways" to your just-previous life or
your just-next future life. This is why it is necessary that each individuated expression of the Higher Self directly connect to the
Higher Self, and in this way it gains access to its other expressions.
Each individuated expression, you see, is sort of "assigned" to a
Higher Self, and all of its multi-dimensional expressions share that
same Higher Self.

We would define "Higher Self" as an aspect of the Core Soul
that has ascended to a point where it has the "ability" to create
seed selves, which is the way the God Source created the higher
beings: the Angelic realm, the great Elders of the planetary systems, and so forth. Thus, there is always this imagined "hierarchi-
cal" structure based on an ability to create greater and greater
manifestations of the Self. Many Higher Selves share the same
Oversoul. There are many Oversouls that "report to" an even
higher entity, and then those are groups as well. This goes on and
on and on. It is very difficult to understand at this level.

What is critical to emphasize here is that the access point to
retrieving information about your other incarnational selves—
past, concurrent (because you have in the same "lifetime" other
expressions of you that are in other parts of the world), and future
selves—is through the Higher Self, always. This is like going to
your mother to get information about your family history. However, it is important not to explore these other expressions of you
merely out of mental curiosity. Do become conscious of the existence of these other expressions of your Higher Self that are your
other multi-dimensional lives, but do not become enamored of
them to the point where you essentially lose your NOW.

It is important to become conscious that they exist. That little spark, itself, makes the energetic values which you term "life issues" or "life lessons" apparent to you: "Ah, I see this has been with me for several lifetimes. Isn't it time to do something about it? Let's resolve this, and then perhaps it will be resolved for another incarnational life as well"—this sort of thing. Here you use the knowledge as a tool for growth and not as an obsession for self-aggrandizement: "I was Napoleon! Aren't I wonderful!"

Our purpose is to have people understand that what would really be optimal to focus on is always ABOVE and not "sideways." Through the direct contact of the Higher Self, yes, you become aware—and should become aware—of your other multi-dimensional expressions, much as your Higher Self is the "mother" of you and your other "siblings." The source, therefore, is the Higher Self, so in that direct contact you allow a consciousness that takes you one step closer to the experience of the ONE. This is the important thing about becoming aware of your other multi-dimensional expressions. It is how they relate to the Higher Self as an act of love and creativity, their having been created to begin with as expressions of the Higher Self so that the Higher Self can learn and grow as well—and that your future is also to become a Higher Self to multi-dimensional expressions!

Sharing Soul Growth

Another factor that may be news to you is that when your consciousness shifts, when you realize something, it affects all your other "selves." As *they* allow a higher consciousness (regarding the dynamic nature of DNA resonance and imprinting), *you* may also allow a higher consciousness. It is the same with your relationship to your other "reincarnational" existences, because when another expression of us . . . we will use ourselves as an example of a "Higher Self": When Jyoti allows a certain consciousness, WE grow! In our growth, we are able to make contact with another expression of us that you might think of as existing in another lifetime of Jyoti Alla-An's. Because of her growth, and then our consequent growth, we are able to contact another expression and awaken it in a way that we were not "able" to do before, and this goes all the way "up" to the God Source level.

Something Jyoti read recently struck her profoundly: "When you deny your own soul growth you deny God's growth." Yes, we are absolutely inter-dependent in this growth process. This is why we feel such joy at these breakthroughs, because it allows us growth. Yes—this thing that you think of as your "little" life impacts the God Source directly when that growth occurs in you—a great way for people to understand that they are totally worthy.

An incarnational expression's negative experiences also affect other lives. Getting involved in so-called "dark" energies does affect your "vertical soul hierarchy" up to the Oversoul level but not beyond that. The reason is that at a point "above" that, the frequency of such "behavior," or vibration, becomes neutralized and balanced. It is not as though if you are "fallen" in one life suddenly the God Source loses some light. At our level, for example (what you term a Higher Self), we would feel this profoundly. In situations such as this we might go in for a "rescue," or another life among your multi-dimensional expressions might become even more "enlightened" to balance this.

A phenomenon similar to negative-entity attachment also occurs *between* lifetimes. If in many lives you have a fear of a certain thing or person, you create a thought form. What you interpret as an entity actually is a limited form or being. It is not a being in a full sense that you have created an entity consciousness—that is capable of plaguing you in several lifetimes simultaneously. You have created the thought-form entity because of the intensity of the fear generated or whatever the other issue is: deprivation, victimization, or whatever.

Consciousness bleed-throughs (which usually occur when a common issue is resonating between multi-dimensional expressions) from other of your incarnational expressions affect you— you feel the impact of other lives. You may suddenly feel very strange and know that it has nothing to do with what's going on in your life here, right now. We would suggest that when you feel this sort of thing coming from you, direct light energy back in the direction from which you're getting the strange energy, and you can help that other expression with whatever s/he is going through. Your intent is enough.

We feel the energy change in that direction, at our level, as a distress signal. Depending on the "time period" in which that expression understands itself to be living, we would send an appropriate emissary. It could be an angel. Sometimes it might be a "demon" to scare people into mending their ways—to scare them into understanding how much they have separated from the One. Again, it is still up to them to get it.

The God Self

(from a public channeling)

PD: What does my Higher Self want of me at this time in my life? I have no clue.

MELORA: Oh, our answer is wonderful news for you. (This is something our Jyoti has been asking about.) You are merging with your Higher Self, so there's a change in your experience of *communication*. Because you are more merged, there isn't a sense of the information/communication coming from a "higher" plane, or from some place outside of you. So all that you're experiencing is that what used to be *communication* is now one with you.

The next step is to be conscious of much more merging with your Higher Self—*being* the Higher Self embodied here. As we spoke of last night [in a monthly public session], Descension is the easier, more elegant way to do it—just letting this happen rather than each individual physical life trying to "pull" itself out of this density. In the recent events of your life, in what you have learned about yourself, what you have released has "made room" for your Higher Self to come in and do more merging with you.

PD: Normally I have tremendous future plans, and it feels that now there really aren't any other than accepting a full-time position that's been offered to me.

MELORA: Virtually all of your answers, and all of your "opera-tions," will be coming more from this source in the future. You will love your work as long as your ego doesn't come in and start analyzing: "Well, this isn't what I want to do," and so on. In awakening personally to the light, each individual on a mission here is coming closer and closer to a conscious understanding of the work they actually came here to do. So there's a time during which there is great conflict (and our Jyoti has experienced this) between personal agenda and the more ego based notion of role, versus the soul-level understanding of mission, on which your entire embodiment is based.

In making that shift between your spiritual work as *you* and how that feels to you, and really committing to the high level of work that you came here to do, you are about at the threshold of that, and so you feel the tug of your personality self saying, "But I want *this* and I want *that*." Understand that the whole purpose of your embodiment and the soul growth that you have desired to allow here depend on moving out of the smaller personality ori-ented issues and into commitment to that work. In many ways, this is what is holding Ascension back. Although the light quo-tient is phenomenal, and many have awakened, you are shifting into the next cycle as we have just described.

PD: I guess the question is: I haven't yet been able to identify the part of me that's the Higher Self communication separate from the part that's the ego. What I keep asking myself is: "Who am I?" because now I am becoming very aware of mergings of time. For moments I can be in two or three places at once. I have visions of landscapes and cities, and I also have visions of moments in past lives. My question is" "Who am I?" I guess you can't answer that huge question, but—

MELORA: Well, actually we can. The identify part is merely the personality part.

PD: Is that the Ego asking the question?

MELORA: Well, for example, *cogito ergo sum*—"I think; therefore I am"—is, of course *the* illusion of 3rd-dimensional consciousness. "I am; therefore I think" would actually be more appropriate, but "Who am I?" is actually a question of the personality. We use this word to show how your Self or Soul is expressed in 3rd-dimensional existence, and if you wanted to think of this on a higher level, personality might be interpreted, for example, as an Ascended Master.

The equivalent of personality as expressed in Ascended Masters and other "self-realized" human beings might appropriately be described as *a quality of energy*—a resonance with a quality or vibration in the upper realms. For example, on the surface, the Lady Master Quan Yin as former "Chohan of the 7th Ray" (or Violet Flame) has a very different resonance than does St. Germain (who is now "Chohan of the 7th Ray"). We think of St. Germain as more of a personality because he is still very much "in touch" with embodiment on the Earth. This makes him such a great emissary in his ascension work with all of you. "Chohan of the 7th Ray" does not limit, or *de*limit, the characteristics of the Ascended Master who holds that so-called job. The resonance of Quan Yin, for example, would be grace, mercy, compassion—very sweet energy. The resonance of St. Germain is much more playful—there is much more of a sense of mischief in addition to the seriousness and adept way in which he works.

The "qualities" of your Soul, your Higher Self, and the other members of your "vertical soul hierarchy" will resonate with you. Whatever your intrinsic nature is—expressed or not—is going to be resonant all the way "up" your soul hierarchy and probably with your personal guides as well. In merging with your Higher Self, your guidance, and so forth (those who are related to you; not merely guides on assignment), you will become even more so.

It may seem to you as if suddenly there is more intensity of those qualities in you, and so the Ego will rise to the occasion. In other words, there is more intensity of your *pure* nature—who you are **as a Soul**—then your Ego will intensify to counteract that, and not *vice-versa*. That's how you distinguish between what's going on with the ego personality expression from what's going on with your Soul, so any sense of resistance is always going to be ego based. Also, whatever experiences of non-love occur are not of your Higher Self. That is another way you can discern what's going on. When you go into meditation now, you are merely *becoming conscious* of a merging that is already taking place.

PD: So the falling asleep part, then . . . just go with that until it comes to conclusion? I thought I was falling asleep because there is something I don't want to hear or know.

MELORA: No. This is an opportunity for many of the calibrations to take place. Understand that when you go into meditation you are really coming into that place of God Self that all share. When you go within yourself you have *Atma*; when you go outside of yourself you have *Brahma*. "*Brahma* and *Atma* are one." In your falling asleep your intention is actually being answered, but if you are fighting falling asleep you would actually be circumventing the setup and merging of certain synaptic pathways necessary while you're still in the physical body. It is like having anesthesia while you're undergoing microsurgery, and in the very act of meditating you are seeking this union and actually allowing it.

Earth Incarnation

(excerpts from a group channeling in Boulder, Colorado)

QUESTIONER 1: I have a question about Indigenous people. Can you tell us more about that? Were we once like that ourselves?

MELORA: If you mean true human beings vs. Starseed, born into human bodies, Starseed incarnate in bodies . . . Those of you who have come to help with the ascension process. You agreed with each other at the Soul level to be what we have described as "S.W.A.T. teams" and to come into embodiment. Not just to "infiltrate," if you will, but also for Soul growth, so that each time you help in a planetary ascension, you allow even more Soul growth. Our Jyoti calls this "getting spiritual brownie points." Then all in your *vertical soul hierarchy* benefit and all of your incarnational lives benefit from this work.

Those you think of as indigenous people go through reincarnation as well, but their origin is not in the stars; it is indeed of the Earth. Thus, there is the Adamic prototype, although Adam was really the same as Jesus. At the Soul level, this was the first prototype for "Man" but Adamic in the sense of being made of the clay of the Earth, both male and female.

Now, other beings come into embodiment not on a mission of ascension at this time, although many or most of those Starseed who are embodied now are on an ascension mission in past times have embodied to learn what is only possible to learn in 3rd Density—what is not possible to learn in a disembodied state. And so it takes great courage to come into embodiment because the density and the risk of forgetting your starry origins or your angelic origins are very great. This is also why there is so much help now. In the past, only a few "escaped," if you will—the few enlightened masters like Buddha. Now, of course, there is the probability of ascension for all, because it is desired by the Creator Source—Prime Creator—to bring everything back in an involutionary manner, or in-breath, not evolutionary, in out-breath fashion.

To recognize indigenous beings is not so easy. We don't have any sort of checklist for you. What we *will* tell you is that their contribution also is very important. They can reach a point of coming out of 3rd-dimensional, incarnational consciousness, just as those who ensouled from star systems and angelic kingdoms have to come out of the 3rd-density consciousness and remember where they came from.

So there *is* growth, just as in the animal kingdom. (Examples are those house pets coming into 3rd-dimensional consciousness, which is self-awareness—consciousness of self—instead of being like animals in the wild with their "hive consciousness". It is like one consciousness.)

Domestic animals that are your friends and companions are doing their work to allow, 3rd-dimensional consciousness. There are many levels within 3rd-dimensional consciousness. They would be the first level of 3rd-dimensional consciousness in their relationship with you.

Just as these animals can evolve out of 2nd-dimensional consciousness, in 3rd, that is true of indigenous humans who are not Starseed, who can travel through the levels "upward," and start coming into 4th-dimensional consciousness. It is just more difficult to do it that way.

QUESTIONER 2: It is a slower process?

MELORA: It is a *much* slower process.

QUESTIONER 3: I have been told by another channel that I have never lived on this Earth before. Is that possible?

MELORA: Oh, that's definitely possible. A person may have had 3rd-dimensional lives in many, infinite numbers of places but not on the Earth, but they also must go through the every-dimensional experience. It just may not be somewhere you would recognize as Earth. There are other star systems, there are other planets, there are other locations where you can experience cause-effect and karma besides the Earth.

Soul Mates

(excerpts from a private session)

QUESTION: What is a Soul Twin?

MELORA: This is *of the same Soul energy source* and would have been decided at the Creator God level—what you term the Higher Self level, which we call the ability to create Seed Selves in 3rd-dimensional reality. It is a sort of experiment, the way twins are separated at birth and find each other after many years. They discover that they have the same food tastes, the same odd way of smiling. All of the creations of Seed Selves are creative expressions of the Higher Self in order to rejoin with the understanding of the Oneness, and this is just another creative way to do it.

The *Soul Mate* is a spiritual essence who has manifested and shared many lives with you, both in the body and not in the body, sharing many adventures intergalactically, if you will, as well, and many spiritual "incarnations," spiritual expressions together in many situations—some 3rd-dimensional, many not. Normally it's a male/female balance that creates this harmonic whole, although if there's a very strong balance already, two of the same sex can come together (if they are balanced female/male within each individual), and that will still express the soul mate relationship. This creates the soul mate recognition you have where you are partners and mates in many expressions—in the body and not in the body—because your resonance is so attractive to each other and your purpose is essentially the same.

QUESTION: Then there could be more than one soul mate?

MELORA: Yes. This has been misunderstood. Your soul mate appropriate to you in this life may be different than the soul mate in another because in each life your resonance is not exactly the same. Even with similarities, there is a unique resonance to each expression. However, you and your *Twin Flame* know each other in every lifetime you are expressing.

CHAPTER THREE:

Cellular Coding/Decoding

(excerpts from a workshop in Sedona, Arizona)

N: I have a question. You mentioned briefly something about re-leasing karma from the DNA. Could you talk a little bit more about that?

MELORA: Yes, and we explained this to someone on the phone recently. All of the archetypal possibilities for your expression, in form, and actually NOT in form, are encoded in your DNA. So we would say, for example, "memories" of your NOT being in form are in your DNA in terms of your connection through the Higher Self to "future" lives, other-dimensional existences, and so forth.

At the DNA level we can replay, or revivify (almost the way you reconstitute freeze-dried food), these programs and turn them into holographic representations of the point in time where we're working. These can be "read" and come to your consciousness, where they can be used like merkabas[10], in a way, in their holographic form rather than in that sort of flat, digital encoding. When the memories go from that linear coding to the holographic, then you're coming into that circular thing that we described in the beginning. Now you have access to all the energies as they flow around, through, about, and so forth.

The reason that Shamanic soul retrieval works at the level that it does is that the shaman is going on a journey and coming into contact, usually, with a visual representation of some archetype, do you see? Some of these archetypes are medicine animals, power animals. These are not to be taken as literally as many think. They're to be seen as messages (as we told S. one time) from the Higher Self to you in a form that is dramatic and that you resonate with and that has meaning for you. If that's power animals, then that's what is selected by your Higher Self as the medium for the message, if you will.

What we're working with [in Higher-Dimensional Soul Retrieval] is the *etheric template*, your perfected blueprint, your perfected energetic structure, your perfected physical body too, all of your other bodies—your higher bodies—and even your CONNECTIONS to your Higher Self, other members of your Soul Group, and so forth. These are all encoded but not all activated. Part of what happens when we do Higher-Dimensional Soul Retrieval is that we energetically transmute karma encodings, as the client is ready to release them.

What you do, for example, when you set your intention to ascend, translates into: "I want to activate these programs so that I can work with them consciously" and so that they come alive instead of being flat (or one-dimensional), digital or linear. They're "puffed up" and spherical and have life, and you can work with them now.

---

[10] "Ascension vehicle": A coherent energy field structured holographically first as a tetrahedron and then evolving into a dodecahedron. Techniques for developing one's personal merkaba are actually taught.

Encoded in your DNA is that you might be a villain in some life-time. You might be a predator; you might be a victim. You might be a hero, or you might be a coward. Every possible scenario of expression, whether it be in a body or as a discarnate spirit, is there for you to work with. In coming into embodiment, you essentially make an intention that you're to play this role, now, in this lifetime, and you call to the template—not just for the physical body but also for the activation of certain scenarios, certain lineages (certain parents), certain childhood teachers, or whatever is going to happen. **You're creating holographic experience, which is what your experience in 3rd Dimension really is.**

However, you're doing it out of your DNA's core programs, which are more infinite than you might imagine. Thus, the perception of scientists that there are these raw genes—and that you inherit these from your mother and father, and so forth, that's your raw material, and that's a static thing—is incorrect because there are ENERGETIC versions of these that run in tandem with, and parallel to, that.

(excerpts from a private session)

Some of the strictures that you think of as karmic issues might not be active things; they might be repressions that you agree to have of certain abilities, certain consciousness levels, or a level of intelligence. You might, for example, choose to have limited intelligence so that you can go more into a spiritual, instead of an intellectual, realm and try that route to allow a higher consciousness. It really is almost like having a dog with a muzzle on it, or a muted trumpet, in the sense of masking certain abilities.

One concept is active and the other is passive. You may have active karmic issues that are very energized, very fierce, and very intense, so that your consciousness is very focused on these. It's like activating lights or turning on an electrical current. The passive might be just to have that muted trumpet or the muzzle on the dog; it's almost like a device that is clamping over or repressing. Either way it's a disallowing of expression or intensifying your experience of something.

On the DNA level, yes, there are certain encodings that activate and certain encodings that restrict, and depending on the personality, the issues will vary. With our Jyoti, for example, the number one issue is freedom, so any restriction placed on her is going to create quite an intense reaction indeed. Instead of muffling her, restriction is going to make her blast that mute right out of the trumpet and probably break your ear drum! She is going to find some way to take that stricture off. This is an expression of a very fierce need in her for freedom.

If you put a muffler on other people they will stay mute. They might suffer from it, and they might internally complain, but they will never try to blast that muffler off of them. Some people will resist intense feeling of any kind. They shrink if anyone expresses anger; they shrink if anyone is direct with them. As a result, they live passive, indirect lives. So, this stricture has an entirely different effect, according to one's personality expression. The same sorts of implants or the same sorts of activated encoding will have a totally different effect on one expression in one lifetime, you see.

One part of the most effective kind of DNA decoding is literally like *translating* an already existing code; another part is *unencoding*, or *removing* certain codes at the DNA level. There would be the intensification of knowledge of decoding at the DNA level being brought to consciousness; then there would be the releasing of that muting kind of implant, the releasing of the inhibitions placed on certain other kinds of information. The result is the same: The information comes to consciousness, brought forth, again, from lifting something that was passively placed there and also resonating in the way you would resonate a tuning fork. Here the information has not been repressed; it is just not able to come to consciousness. So we resonate it, and then you hear it, you perceive it, you experience it.

This process proceeds in layers, each rising to the top and being skimmed (the way you skim leaves off a swimming pool), and then what is beneath is allowed to rise. Until you really have that "last" layer rising to the top, there is always work to be done in the actual decoding process.

Our Jyoti has sensed that multi-dimensional lives share DNA memories in a dynamic way—that energetic strands may connect them. This is how one is able to remember those other lives. There are many parallels to the process of soul retrieval as described in the bringing to resonance of the soul fragment and the Core Soul. The same is true in the interconnections of "reincarnational" lives. Again, this is all on the energetic level.

Just as any experience leaves an impression on you at the DNA-level and the etheric level, on the cellular level there may be transmitted genetically to your progeny the same energetic imprints that can be shared between incarnational lives in the manner that we described earlier—through the resonance of the intensity of the issue to the Higher Self. As you can see, those issues can be experienced, can prevail, across the spectrum of lives, into the future and into the past. Until these issues are resolved, they resonate quite intensely indeed in several simultaneous life expressions.

Even one's ability to manifest abundance may be inhibited at the DNA level. You are limited by the coding of the DNA. (Incidentally, the reconnection of the 12 strands of DNA has more to do with opening vaster *communication* channels to relationships on the higher soul level, enabling light communication to reach you and open your consciousness to vaster light values and letting the body absorb much greater light values.) The encoding is in the form of limitations, which you may have read about as "implants" of sorts that inhibit certain abilities. According to the human belief and experience of what you call "karma," you might come into this life having chosen to inhibit abilities in order to create challenges for yourself to overcome and to learn the karmic lessons for which you embodied.

This is why doing cellular decoding work is so beneficial to the ascension process. In the decoding process it is much as if a scientist touches part of the brain with an electrode. You experience something from the past in a holographic manner: smell, touch, taste, sight, hearing. In the cellular release of the encoding, you see, the "memories" of your lives may be revisited, much as when you "see [your] life flash before your eyes" before a death, or near-death, experience.

Soul retrieval and multi-incarnational merging are other important methods of releasing "karmic" influences. Merging consciously with other incarnational lives is just as important as retrieving lost soul aspects from this life, for if you remain unconscious of incarnational lives, you bring their issues (which are also your issues) to your "next" incarnation. Life issues on which you've worked seemingly "forever" without success often indicate consciousness "bleed-throughs" from other lives.

One benefit of tapping in to your other incarnational lives is that you can recapture the energetic imprint of the positive experiences and skills expressed in those other lives. For example, if you were a wonderful horseback rider, say, on the Steppes of Russia. In suggesting to yourself in this expression of you that you wish to remember those abilities as a rider in that life, you could actually recapture those abilities and "suddenly" be a crack rider now. **The energetic (or experiential) values are the vehicles for bringing forth talents and experience from one life to another in the form of DNA. Those values are the ones that survive the destruction of the physical body.**

Understand that the *experiential values* one gleans from each lifetime are what are encoded in the DNA. In the decoding process the "karmic" memories are exposed for what they are, brought to the consciousness in a sort of holographic recreation. After her own decoding work, Jyoti sensed that the decoding process is two-fold: One part is literally decoding (or translating an already existing code); the other part is un-encoding, or removing certain codes at the DNA level. Thus, the decoding is an intensification of knowledge that the coding exists at the DNA-level—i.e., this knowledge is brought to an individual's consciousness. The un-encoding would be the releasing of a kind of implant that suppresses the consciousness of certain kinds of information.

During the decoding process the etheric blueprint is cleared of "programming" from the current life and from other lives. The cells are infused with more light (photons) so that every single atom starts to vibrate at a higher frequency and dormant parts of the DNA become activated. When the DNA is awakened, realigned and evolved, you no longer have to keep experiencing issues from the past.

A Glimpse into Ancient Egypt

(excerpts from a private session after the author's decoding experience)

Jyoti saw images of the Egyptian pyramids under blue moonlight, and the Sphinx when it was new, and the ankh being impressed energetically on the third eye. Were these memories, or were they just knowledge brought to her with the initiation?

MELORA: They are both. Picture an incarnational experience in ancient Egypt in which our Jyoti was led into the Great Pyramid, which really was an initiatory structure—not a tomb, not a place of worship—and picture that Jyoti went through a very rigorous initiation (years, and years, and years of initiatory levels in this structure) in a very ancient time that precedes even the Egyptian mysteries of Akhenaton, who came much later. Picture her in this structure almost at the very beginning of its, and the Sphinx's, existence. In going through the initiation rights, she connects with all of her multi-dimensional selves, including *this* one, which, at that time, would have been seen as a future self.

In the decoding initiation by The Great White Brotherhood (as you know the ankh is part of their emblem—it is more than just the symbol of life; it is an energetic *key* into communication), she saw the pyramids, the blue moonlight and the sphinx, and saw the ankh being energetically impressed on her third eye. She connected directly to that so-called "past" life. In that same moment they experienced each other. Her sense that the blue moonlight was from the second moon that has been referred to in *You Are Becoming a Galactic Human*[11] . . . that book is correct. Before this moon was used as a projectile of destruction there were two

---

[11] *You Are Becoming a Galactic Human*, by Virginia Essene and Sheldon Nidle. S E E Pub, 1994. 237 pages.

moons, and the moon that Jyoti saw in her initiation indeed shone blue moonlight on the pyramids.

The two moons achieved fullness at about the same time, and so you had this stark white moonlight and then the blue moonlight, which really are the resonances of the third eye energy. At that time, that was the consciousness of those who inhabited that part of the planet, and so the very resonance of the blue moonlight and the beautiful white moonlight were parts of the levels of frequencies that were established to help promote and maintain the high frequency vibration of the beings at that time. As you know, that frequency has degenerated fairly completely.

About what date was that?

MELORA: The date was 97,350 B.C. The ankh is a conscious connection to the most ancient derivation of the symbol—the initiatory connection between humanity and the God Source in a total experience of communication. This is its truest meaning.

CHAPTER FOUR:

Choosing Incarnational Life Circumstances

(excerpts from a private session)

SW: Jyoti asks, "When we choose an incarnational existence, do we choose the whole *gestalt* of it? Or do we choose particular aspects of that embodiment? The example is, when one chooses to come into incarnation with the 2nd chakra open—so that you can explore clairsentience—the trouble is, with the 2nd chakra open, it attracts sexual predation."

MELORA: Yes.

SW: Now, the choice was made to have the 2nd chakra open and then, in doing that, you put up with what comes with the package? Is that what you're saying?

MELORA: Give us a moment. There is a mixed answer to this. We would say that, for the most part, what is chosen is the gestalt of that physical incarnation, so it means: "What is the more generic setup, and what are the challenges and issues to be explored?" You come into incarnation with the 2nd chakra open, as an example, to experience *clairsentience*, and what you wish between embodiments is to learn how to master your life on Earth with abilities that are greater than those of most around you in terms of reading energies and even reading people's thoughts. The real challenge that you have chosen is to master the reality, do you see—to master physical incarnation with special gifts that are beyond most people's, which is understood by the entity incarnating to be even more difficult than is basic incarnation. That is what you have chosen.

So there is a sense, or an understanding, that harm—in many forms—may come to you as a result of this but not a specific understanding that harm can come to you in the form of sexual abuse (or, in the case of Salem, Massachusetts, for example, being burned as a witch). There is almost a pure energetic understanding that harm may come to you, but you still choose to do that.

SW: Okay. Again, this goes back to my question of a long time ago: "Who's in charge?" Does the person who's incarnating design with High Self and Oversoul, or whatever, that in this embodiment the 2nd chakra will be open? Then it is so?

MELORA: Yes, and the trouble you may be having in understanding here is the now-prevalent belief in the statement, for example, in *Seth Speaks*[12]: "You create your own reality." We're not saying

---

[12] *Seth Speaks: The Eternal Validity of the Soul*, by Jane Roberts. Prentice-Hall, Inc., 1972. 445 pages.

that this is not true; what we're saying is that (and even Seth talked about the many possible parallel selves that you have, depending on which turns in the road you take) the number of variables is enormous. In the flow of your life you pick variable number 60,235,000 and whatever . . . and then you turn in some direction that could not have been predicted before you came into incarnation. Do you understand why we just said this?

SW: So that's the free will? That's the part of the choices of being embodied?

MELORA: Right, and in the flow of time and circumstance, and in the interaction with other beings, there are so many variables that there's no way you would have known before you came into incarnation that in 1966, July 30th, at 2:37 p.m. you would fall off a cliff and break your leg.

SW: Um hmm. You know, one thing I was just thinking about: If this embodiment, if I chose (like Jyoti says in her question) to have my the 2nd chakra open, is it possible to have six other embodiments, parallel to this one, that are working on each of the other major chakras?

MELORA: We are seeing that this would be rather unusual, and also that it wouldn't make much sense. For example, most incarnate beings are oriented around the 1st and 2nd chakras and up to the navel chakra. (The 1st chakra and the navel chakra hold fear-based energies. These are about your physical survival and perpetuation issues, etc.) The great difference between this Age and those of all past ages is that you are cultivating the heart chakra and the chakras above it. We are seeing that there would be more possibility of individuals trying to have all their chakras open and balanced than what you described.

SW: Okay.

MELORA: And did you have other questions besides the one Jyoti asked, regarding this subject?

SW: I thought your answer was interesting because the ideal would be that you decide to come in and have your 2nd chakra open in this incarnation, for whatever varying experience it happens to bring. Then you deal with what comes up in knowing that that's what you chose.

MELORA: Yes, but the other thing is that you could also turn into a person who just loves to have sex all the time and who really enjoys it. That doesn't always happen—that you come in being clairsentient and just enjoy physical life much more. So that's a possibility too.

SW: Thank you, Melora.

CHAPTER FIVE:

"Walk-Ins"

Melora notes that it's the walk-in who benefits when beings agree to this—not the one walked in to—because having the walk-in take on the current lifetime of karma prevents the Soul growth of the one walked in to. According to Melora, that karma still has to be worked through in the "future" incarnations of that being. So the benefit to the one walking in is that it can get down to business right away in an adult body and not have to go through the birth, early childhood, adolescence and young adult process of forgetting, developing and then maybe not remembering the business it wants to do.

Melora has stated that she perceives the walk-in as USING the embodied being. It is moot that permission is given because the walk-in entity gets all the advantages. The walked-in-to entity just gets some respite from some current business of the Soul. If the walked-in-to being/body were really finished with its karma, it would ascend, much as when great gurus take maha samadhi[13]. *They would live out their lives in service to the Divine and go through physical death. If the new inhabitant, and the original body inhabitant/personality, are both parts of the original consciousness or Soul Group, this would make more sense to me. Then this is NOT a walk-in situation. It is merely a merging of other parts of the Core Soul unit.*

(excerpts from a private session)

SW: Jyoti wanted to know more about walk-ins. She said that you, Melora, don't particularly approve of walk-ins and wanted you to comment on this.

MELORA: We would say that we are not resonant with that, or, to be more accurate, that we find it inappropriate to Soul growth or inhibitive of true Soul growth.

We're seeing that the agreement is at the Higher Self level, not above. It is not even at the Soul level. An entity not of your Soul lineage—but who wants to come into incarnation without having to go through the birth process, the learning process, and all of that—speaks to the consciousness of the embodied entity (often-times in the dream state) and says, "I see you're really having a hard time. I can let you off the hook here. I will live out your karma." (It's not always explicitly stated, but it's only the karma in the current lifetime—not the karma before and not the karma after. It's only the karma accrued in the current lifetime, which everybody thinks is such a great deal, but it's not.) "I will live out the karma of your current lifetime, and you can take off and not have to be in this body anymore." However, this is like a tempo-rary reprieve, and that consciousness or that being still has to come back into another body at some point to live out what it was supposed to learn when it came into the current-lifetime body.

---

[13] In Hinduism, the achievement of permanent sameness or identity with the object of meditation (God)—but with death of the physical body.

SW: Okay. Well, again, that brings me back to the question: "Who's in charge?" Apparently, from what you've said, it's the High Self and not necessarily on the Soul level.

MELORA: It is permitted through the High Self but it is actually initiated by the consciousness of the person embodied. The Higher Self doesn't say: "Okay. I'll let the walk-in come in." This thought is actually initiated by the embodied entity, and the Higher Self says, "Well, okay. If you must, you must." Free will.

SW: The other question I've got that is sort of related to this is whether reincarnation in the same body is possible.

MELORA: It is not necessary to do it that way. You can also have simultaneous lives so, as *in The Seth Material*[14] that was so brilliantly and clearly brought in by Jane Roberts, you have possible selves that are living out lifetime choices that you didn't live out. You have possible selves; you have concurrent lives. Some say you have a pod of 6 to 12 concurrent embodiments on the Earth and that it's possible to meet and recognize them. So why would you need to reincarnate in the same body?

Again, what we're hearing is that these are misinterpretations. To be a clear channel or to be linking clearly, sometimes you have to wait long enough to make sure you're getting the really specific and accurate version of the energetic information. We call this "energy information packets." Writing would be a good parallel to use: Good writers don't settle for the first thing they hear in their minds. They say to themselves: "Okay, what do I really mean?" It might take them an hour to think of the one word in a poem that really conveys their intention, and they can't be lazy about it. In order to be really accurate you sometimes have to search. You can't say the first thing that comes to your mind just so that you can move on to the next thing.

---

[14] *The Seth Material*, by Jane Roberts. Bantam Books, 1981. 304 pages.

When some people bring in information they'll get the *energy information packet* of very complex answers (such as the way we work when we're answering your questions), and they will settle on the first thing they "see" or "hear." Actually the answer is maybe two or three below that or under that or behind that.

SW: Like reading between the lines?

MELORA: Or just waiting until the resonance says, "No, that's not it but I'm getting closer. Oh. This is it." People who are clairvoyant often have the worst problem of distortion because they see an image and they take it literally, but they often change what they're seeing because it's going through the egoistic mechanism. It's much like when you're dreaming, and in the dream it makes sense but after you wake up and remember it, it seems really ludicrous. While you're dreaming it you know exactly what it means, but when you try to tell someone else about it, your mind reinterprets it to fit 3rd-dimensional "reality," and then it loses its original impact and meaning. **What the clairvoyant sees is <u>already</u> a *reinterpretation* of the energetic message that came in**, so then the egoistic structure tries to make sense of it in 3-D, and then it gets changed forever in ways purely energetic information that came in would not have changed.

CHAPTER SIX:

Soul Transplants

(excerpts from a private session)

PD: A friend of mine says she's a "soul transplant" and would like to know her new spiritual name.

MELORA: Yes, and as your friend said, soul transplants are not walk-ins. It's almost like transplanting your own heart back into your own body from the past, when it was healthy, into the future when it "became" unhealthy. This is very difficult to describe, and we haven't been asked this question before.

We're seeing that a soul transplant occurs as a result of getting into a sort of soul-weary state. The soul starts wandering around (almost the way you saw our Jyoti's Light Body wandering around in another universe), and it gets really dissociated. If the soul comes from a high enough level, originally—say, it is star seeded—often times it is taken to a higher-dimensional "place" and sort of re-educated.

However, what's tricky about the process, and what makes it a transplant, is that there's a going-back-in-time or going-to-the-future sort of thing going on with the Soul itself. There's a temporary detachment from the body and then a sort of "hospital" stay for the Soul to bring it back to health, as you might term it. Then it is actually reattached into the body, if this makes sense. This is what we're seeing, and it's very odd to us.

PD: With cords of attachment?

MELORA: Well, in the way the soul is always in the body. It requires all of the bodies—not just the physical body. "Re-attachment" is the only word we can think of. It's not physically attached; it's energetically attached. It's a re-association and re-enlivening of all the bodies from within, as the Soul is brought back into the central energetic core, re-creating the integrity of all of those bodies.

PD: Coming into an alignment?

MELORA: But the Soul actually is moved from the bodies. It is like being temporarily put on life support at the Soul level. There's a vacating of the body, and then the Soul is just taken to a place where it's sort of renovated and then re-associated with all the bodies—[meaning the physical body and the higher bodies, such as the mental, emotional, etheric, kethric, astral and spiritual bodies]. Your friend was correct in saying that it's not the same thing as a walk-in.

PD: Does a soul transplant provide access to higher information or more awareness? Or is it so subtle that the entity is unaware of it?

MELORA: It's not subtle. It's almost the same as when people who are abducted say they lost two hours of time, and they don't know where the time went. They're aware that they lost time. It's not exactly traumatic, but the person is aware that something has been missing, that there's been a shift. This is really done at the request of the Higher Self because sometimes when there's a problem with the soul substance as it enlivens an incarnational expression, that soul substance becomes obliterated. It's considered lost forever and must start over.

Actually, we should say that this is a choice at the Core Soul level to redo certain things, and then the person is actually where s/he started, at a certain point, before things began to go awry. That is the sense of going forward in time, then bringing that back into a time when it was still okay. Within the consciousness, it gives you a sort of second chance. This could not happen if there were any karmic repercussions. This is not a karmic consideration; this is just simply a choice about the direction of consciousness, and it feels like you have a bad carburetor or something at the soul level. It's like: "This is not really fair, so we have to reinstate this as a brand-new condition"—or the condition as it existed before the carburetor went bad.

This situation has not been very prevalent before now. Let us see if this is going on more currently. We see this as more of an exception, so we're not sure if your friend thinks this is something that is going on a lot now. However, we're not seeing that this sort of thing is going on that much. It's most interesting.

Let us now go to the question about your friend's "new" name. Her interpretation is, as a soul transplant, that she has a new spiritual name. Really what's going on is the sense of being repaired—or re-established in a state where she's normal again.

Whereas, now, in her own consciousness, she can maintain that, she couldn't before. However, her impression is that she's new, that she's a new person or a new soul. Now, she's been told that she has a new name, so let us see if we can figure out what that interpretation might be so that we can help her with that. Give us a moment. Oh. It is that she has her original name, which changed as the carburetor went bad, so to speak. She was unable to re-member or perceive her true name, which now she can. So in that sense it's a new name. We figured that it was something tricky like that. We are receiving "Astra-la."

CHAPTER SEVEN:

Soul Groups—Your Soul Niche

Following are Melora's explanations of what soul groups are, how we (as embodiments) are related to our Higher Self, and what our purpose is in relationship to the other members of our soul group.

We are indeed Melora, and we wish to introduce a new way of looking at what you term "soul groups." A soul group would be all your various selves, a group organized "under" what you would term as one Oversoul, Higher Self, all your multi-dimensional seed selves (past, present and future), the fragmented soul aspects, infinite numbers of possible selves, and so on. This is ongoing. Perhaps it seems to you that there is a sort of finite point at which these things end—and that you can then count them all and say, "There are *this* many, and this is when they ascend." Actually you experience soul groups in 3rd-dimensional reality in a multi-dimensional fashion.

Each multi-dimensional "self" has a separate consciousness—individuated out of the One, as we are when we come to you. All are "tied together" in consciousness, and so when we say that we are an "individuated" being, it is a manifestation that "steps out," if you will, of the consciousness of The One and that expresses itself as a "personality." (This is so that on this plane people will recognize us and because you need answers to such questions as "Who are you?" and "What is your name?" and "What message do you bring?") We are an individuated consciousness as an expression of The One, one of the infinitudes of expressions of The One that you call the Universe—all of the inhabitants, and all of the stars and planets in it, and all of the creations that express it.

Soul Groups go through an Ascension process together. So that you can perceive and understand this process, we will ask you to picture little hatch marks lined up in several tiers, in several levels, although it is not that simple. If you remember that the process of Ascension is ongoing—and that it always has been, always will be—it will seem more like moving up and up and up in "rows." As many of you as there are in your soul group, there are as many of us; and as many of us as there are, there are as many higher under which we are "collected," much as a Higher Self is related to an Oversoul.

Understand that there are many Higher Selves "reporting to" that Oversoul, so just at that level of one Oversoul, you have many Higher Selves "reporting to" that Oversoul. For each Higher Self there are many members of the soul group "reporting to" that Higher Self, and for each member of the soul group there are multi-dimensional [reincarnational] lives "reporting to" that member of the soul group. Then for each multi-dimensional life there are soul fragments that need to be brought back. (Merging with the Higher Self requires the soul integration process of returning these "lost" soul aspects.) In each multi-dimensional life—

what you would term a "reincarnational" life—there are soul aspects of other beings sharing each of those "past" lives with you. There are also "future" and "present" lives. You can look at the members of the soul group to which you belong as "soul fragments" to us.

So many of you now working with ascension seem to be interpreting that the process will take place just with you—just with your body in this lifetime. (It's not just "little ol' me," as Jyoti says, "leaving this life and ascending.") The problem with this view is that it doesn't account for karma: what you share with other expressions of your multi-dimensional Self. In the work that we do with soul retrieval we are bringing as many other of the incarnational expressions back to the Higher Self as possible.

Ascension is consciousness of your multi-dimensional selves, of soul aspects that need to be brought back, of other members of your soul group, of higher guides who are parts of your Higher Self, and so forth. Some have asked whether ascension is also a merging into the Oversoul, a merging of all the multi-dimensional selves. Your experience of your Oversoul will not occur until you have done the same sort of "work" that we have been doing, so that the entire group can ascend. But, again, **what you are conscious of determines your experience of that ascension.** Now, there is not just one ascension agenda, not just one soul growth agenda for everyone. Building the merkaba vehicle is not necessary for everyone. Some people ascend by following in consciousness right to their guides; some do it by letting the Higher Self merge with them in the body, then the Oversoul as well, which is called *Descension*. This is easier than Ascension!

This is what such great enlightened beings as Buddha have done. They have let the "vertical soul hierarchy" descend and merge with them while they're in the body. Buddha integrated all of his incarnational lives while he was in the body. He became the predominant consciousness while in the body. That is the greatness of his achievement in enlightenment through the mind.

Eventually you expand in consciousness to the point where you know that there is only the One; you have no consciousness of duality. Remember: It is only separation from the One in consciousness that makes any being not understand or experience, the Oneness. *We* are fully aware that Oneness exists, but it is not in our energetic experience fully. We merely have different "tools" at our disposal when our consciousness expands, and when we ascend "higher" (we say "wider," "bigger").

The beginning of the Aquarian Age (this new millennium and the ten years or so following) just happens to provide portals of maximized opportunities for ALL in a soul group. It creates the sense of urgency you all are feeling and it is what compels you to take advantage of the acceleration that is possible in this time.

The Author's Soul Group

(excerpts from a private session)

GD: You mentioned that you, as Melora, resonate more strongly with the soul group with whom Jyoti Alla-An embodied in ancient Greece. Does that mean that Jyoti has other soul groups and that you might be part of other soul groups as well?

MELORA: You have actually explained it rather well. In claiming that we resonate more to that *wing* of her soul group in Classical Greece we were expressing that the work we are doing with ascension in this dimension at this "time" in the simultaneity of ALL—as we focus our consciousness here to do this work—the resonance is with the quality of consciousness connection we also have with her "now." In other words, the resonances in her expression in classical Greece and now are very similar. (Jyoti was an apprentice to an embodiment of Pallas Athena on Crete in pre-classical times and a high priestess to Athena in classical Greece. Jyoti understands that high priestesses were really channels of the goddess energy: The goddess spoke through the high priestess to the people and embodied through the high priestess.)

The resonance is so almost exact that these parallel lives are able to merge in consciousness, and there is great power. It's like having a direct pipeline through Time, connecting Jyoti's experience in these ancient lives with this one now. Since the work is about merging, and since these qualities of connection are the same, the power in the connection now is similar to that of the ancient expression. The bridges are tremendous and total—"back," "through," and "across," as you would put it—to those times. We perceive that you know this is a multi-dimensional, not just a three-dimensional, kind of spherical or geometrical-energetic relationship here. It's as when you touch one part of a spider's web and the whole web vibrates. In setting up this pipeline, and in suggesting that we are more resonant with that wing of her soul group incarnate in classical Greece, we're saying that across the simultaneous lives, this has the most power to resonate more dimensionality in consciousness than any other soul group that you would also think of as existing, each in its own "niche."

How Jyoti came to our affiliation with her is difficult to explain. This idea was originally presented to Jyoti through another channel whose guide said that we gave the name "Melora" to clue Jyoti into that particular life in which she was singing and playing the part of Helen of Troy in the Acropolis amphitheater[15]. In her becoming conscious of that life and starting to resonate in her understanding of what went on then, and as a priestess in other times, her more artistic and creative work in classical Greece resonates across her lives most profoundly.

She can do even greater work here, however, in this life. Looking back from what you consider to be the future, those lives continuously draw upon each other. Thus, the more power you have here, the more power they have there, because it's simultaneous. This is the resonance that makes it possible and that accelerates the process of merging that we wish to result in consciousness for what Jyoti calls her "vertical soul hierarchy." Understand that it is an access for (and *axis of*, if you will) each part of what you might see as a gyroscope.

---

[15] I re-experienced this lifetime during a hypnotic regression in 1985.

GD: So who IS Melora? You have said that you are "one of The Council of Four," including Pallas Athena. You've said that you are directed by The Council of Four and, at other times, *are* The Council of Four or on the Council of Four. We know there are numerous councils and that sometimes we are members of more than one council.

MELORA: Our introduction of the concept of "The Council of Four" was to help explain a composite resonance and the "work," as you would describe it, that we are doing—in terms of Jyoti's remembrance of her lineage, her understanding of her own pivotal role in this work in anchoring consciousnesses from "way up here." People might say: "Now wait a minute! There's a Council of Five"; "There's a Council of Twelve," and so on. As these rigid structures are being placed on it, the explanation breaks down.

It is a sort of description, a particularization, that really doesn't exist "here" at all, so you might think of The Council of Four as a subcommittee of a greater committee, but the way we think of it is that The Council of Four is of the Oneness; we resonate together as you do as friends. We "hang out" together because of similar talents, energies and "mission," and because of our interest in clear communication, beauty and truth, and so on. For example, we also do the work that Athena "did" in The Temple of Truth in Atlantis. (According to Dr. Joshua David Stone[16], like the Lady Master Quan Yin, Pallas Athena is on the Karmic Board.)

Although our resonances are similar, it's not as though we have coffee together and discuss these things intellectually. Our energy is drawn in the direction of what resonates with us, and the impulse to merge in the light is very strong in us. The resonance of the members of this council is so similar that we feel pleasure in mingling our energies and in expressing ourselves together because when your energies are combined it is more than just double—it is exponential. So you can see that we have come together as beings and composites, soul collectives, consciousness collec-

---

16 *Beyond Ascension: How to Complete the Seven Levels of Initiation,* by Joshua David Stone, Ph.D. Light Technology Publishing, 1995. 280 pages.

tives, groups, whatever, because of the sheer joy of expressing and sharing our energies together and of experiencing the compounding of that resonance.

Therefore, yes—it is like coming from the center of this sphere—or we will put it another way: Throw a pebble into the still water and the rings move out from the center in the ecstatic waves of energy that we experience. So there's much joy and pleasure in this. It is not as though we're doing this, as you would say "just out of the goodness of our hearts." We seek the ecstatic experience of this energy, the exponential increases in resonance.[17]

GD: You refer to yourself as "ourselves." Are you, in fact, a group energy?

MELORA: You could think of us, Melora, as a collective that is in the process of becoming an even greater collective that will include Pallas Athena and the other members of the council, and many others, in what you term "the future." In her most ancient Earth embodiment Athena was authentically an avatar, and that is why the worship of Athena was so strong. That is why such great structures were erected to her, and that is why her energy is still able to be in the statues—because she was a being embodied on the earth—not just a concept, not just channeling through someone from a disembodied state.

So you can see that in the other "reincarnational lives" there would be such great resonance, because the consciousness is, "This is a living entity," and there is that anchor experience of Athena in the body. You remember that she is a real being. When she was embodied as an avatar she was also simultaneously in other dimensions, in other roles as a guide, as a goddess, as an Ascended Master . . . but also in the body for the purpose of anchoring all of that consciousness and all the other expressions of her (from the "highest" to the "lowest") while she was in the body and having that merging.

---

17 For more on The Council of Four, see Appendix A.

GD: So there are many here on earth who are connected to each of THE FOUR?

MELORA: Yes. The subgroups, if you will. There is the soul group, for example, that resonates across time through various incarnations in classical and pre-classical Greece, because the consciousness was so tuned-in, and our relationship in consciousness in that way allowed the consciousness in that soul group. There are other soul groups that you would think of as "subgroups" to various members of The Council of Four whose purpose is not in specific resonance with that lineage of the ancient Greece group. In other words, that purpose is not the most pervasive consciousness connection for them.

GD: And yet some of us, down here, may be aware of connecting through those groups?

MELORA: Yes, and of being "members" of those other soul groups.

GD: So this entire group, now, as a unit, has a specific purpose?

MELORA: **A good way to answer this is to say that in being aware of specific past lives, such as in Pompeii or during the Renaissance, for example, there will always be a similar motif in each of the past lives that you are all remembering the most intensely as a group.** If you think of the Renaissance as a time of the greatest flowering of the arts (next to that of classical Greece), and so on, you start to see what is similar in the soul group's expression, experience and consciousness. Thus, perhaps another "wing" of the soul group is more tuned-in to the Renaissance time than it is to ancient Greece. That whole group is also in Paris at the time of the Impressionist painters, and they are in other cultures in which the arts and literature flourish, because in that particular wing they are really intensively playing out the art aspect—the artistic, creative . . . literally in writing, painting, singing, playing music, and so on. This remains resonant with The Council of Four.

Another group are revolutionaries fighting for freedom and truth, which is another expression of the main "issues" of The Council of Four. Others are great orators, writers, communicators and statesmen in the true sense of the word, as in the founding fathers of America. They, too, are expressing freedom, but the intensity of expression goes into cratory and communication. These, too, are main issues explored by The Council of Four.

GD: Are you saying that all of these things that we might consider to be in the past are all being now brought to the fore, in the present, now, as a part of the main purpose of The Council of Four?

MELORA: Yes, and we wish to say that Jyoti's latching on to Jean Houston's term "polyphrenic"[18] is very important here, as you can see that the more conscious you are of other lives the more you're seeing that, throughout these many lifetimes, all of these parallel existences are expressing the same motifs but, maybe, choosing to express one more than the other, as in painting. However, your love of freedom, the necessity for you to have the truth, your requirement for beauty, cross all the dimensional existences.

So, you see, in certain periods of "history" there is more opportunity to express certain aspects of this. For example, the time of the American Revolution was not known as a great time for the arts in America. [laughs] In embodying in certain "periods" of history, the soul expression is selecting a life in which it can experience that aspect more fully, can focus more on that aspect, and

---

18 *A Mythic Life: Learning to Live Our Greater Story*, by Jean Houston. Harper, 1997. 352 pages. In part of this book the spiritual psychologist explores synchronistic events that brought her to consciousness of her Soul connection with Athena: "What . . . I call Athena may be the archetypal source of the Essence of similar incarnations. In other words, we of the family of Athena are being spored with similar energies and styles to help the archetypal person or greater *daimon* [Gr., *divine power*] with 'her' unfolding in the world of space and time."

can enhance the necessity for experiencing many different lives in different countries and in many different times in history.

Classical Greek, as a Language

I have questions concerning the Greek language. My guide mentioned some time ago that there are certain concepts that can be brought in through the Greek language that we don't have words for in the English language. Is that because of the tonals or is it something else?

We understand this to be more a matter of the association of the information memory from the life, much as we spoke of soul fragments being stuck in time and having consciousness only of what was going on when they "left." Having been expressed and thought in that language, the values, memories and associations with that are more directly and readily accessible, and are sort of resonated, or triggered, by the very words in which they were expressed and thought.

So it's not just the limitations of the English language? Just a familiarity with the sound of ancient Greek?

Familiarity with the sound of the Greek is a great part of it. But there are idioms that are very difficult to translate—that do not have equivalents in English precise enough to express certain concepts, but that is the smaller part. You could do the same thing by saying: "I am now going to channel myself from that life," and then, even if you heard it in Greek and didn't understand it with your mind, now, speaking English, the higher-consciousness level that is telepathic (in which concepts are communicated without words), you would still be getting the meaning even though you're hearing it in Greek. You'd be translating between lives telepathically. This is the way we "channel." We do not speak *to* our Jyoti; we come through her energetically and her brain translates our "language" into words by way of what we call "energy information packets."

CHAPTER EIGHT:

Soul Assignments

(excerpts from a private session)

MELORA: Soul Assignments are group shared, are *Soul Group* shared, and they originate with the being most highly evolved of that Soul Group. If we use Athena as an example (who she is in her most exalted and most evolved expression), we can explain that Soul Assignments regard your resonance, which we have explained before—what issues or aspects of [3rd-dimensional] reality that the group wishes to explore in its many expressions, whether that's physical, just energy, or whatever that is. Whatever dimensions, whatever universes. ("Issues" would be the Earth term, meaning that in Earth embodiment that would be an issue or a challenge. "Aspects of reality" would be the Soul-level term.)

Those qualities are what enable Ascended Beings to distinguish each other from each other, even though they are in Oneness consciousness. Because of this, someone of the Order of Melchizedek[19] would be able to recognize a Christed Being, even in the Oneness consciousness. **There is not any evolved being or god, no matter how evolved, that is totally whole. That's what creates Infinity.** That movement toward wholeness creates and moves into Infinity. This is a very important understanding. Therefore, one of the first clues on Earth that a person is not enlightened is when they say: "I am enlightened." Do you see?

SW: [laughs] Yes because a kahuna I was working with said, "Kahunas don't call themselves 'kahuna'; other people do." Do soul groups vary in size?

MELORA: Oh, of course. This would range not even according to time. It would vary according to that seeding—that concept of seeding consciousness, as in Starseed. There are "older" or more

---

[19] *Melchizedek* is actually a title, as in *Christos* ("Christ consciousness"). This title means that beings have attained a certain quality of enlightened consciousness and belong to specific Melchizedek orders of The Great White Brotherhood. Some, as priests, actually are embodied on the Earth at various times. Most serve as guides from higher dimensions. (The author is of the Priesthood of Melchizedek.) According to *EaTrom*: "This Order is considered to be of the Highest Order of Spirituality. Beyond or outside the functions of man and government... or even 'organized religion' . . . the beliefs that once one accepts the Priesthood, that one is considered a Priest throughout all incarnations."
(http://www.blazing-trails.com/LightWorkers/melchizedek.html)
Also: "The groups affiliated with the Melchizedek teachings are quite broad in orientation. Virtually all are concerned with the advancement of consciousness, the connection of the heaven and earth polarities via the merkabah (flower of life globe-like structure found around all life forms), and the science of the grid work system of the universe. Each group is interested in a slightly different aspect of this broad field."
(http://www.crystallife.com/home/Links.htm)

ancient groups, and we're not talking millennia; we're talking trillions of years. You could conceivably talk about a *core* group of beings that existed—not one, but at least two. Not ever one. You could probably get to that point, but their evolution from where they started has so many permutations that it's like fractals. That's why there can't be One God—ever. That's why the Yahweh of *Genesis* is not the same as the Yahweh of *Ecclesiastes*—because Yahweh keeps evolving.

SW: Yes. Like we do. Of course.

MELORA: That's why our Jyoti put her question in parentheses ("The Yahweh of the Old Testament?") Continuing to impose those static structures on Yahweh on Earth can hold people back from their own evolution.

SW: So Jyoti's Soul Group is huge?

MELORA: Yes—

SW: I was wondering if you could measure it on one hand or two.

MELORA: [laughs] This is very brilliant on the part of the guide of another channel she works with. He said that we could be termed as residing in Classical Greek times in the body as females, as priestesses, and so forth. That wing of the Soul Group is what we termed as Melora.

SW: Right. So you are a grouping—

MELORA: We are a wing of the much, much larger Soul Group, so our group consciousness could be considered one wing, if you will, of the much larger Soul Assignment group.

SW: Are you in contact with the other wing?

MELORA: At the Athena level, yes.

SW: So Athena really can access the other wing?

MELORA: Yes. Exactly.

SW: And then she could pass that information to Jyoti?

MELORA: Yes.

SW: Would that be helpful or would it be overwhelming?

MELORA: We wouldn't be able to do that right now, but we *will* be able to do that, yes. So we are our Jyoti's point of access, if you will, to that source, Athena, as the highest member of that Soul Assignment that can contact our Jyoti through us.

SW: But there are things out there, just like the writing on the mountain for the Jews—there are things out there that Jyoti would not be able to comprehend at this time?

MELORA: . . . because that is not her lineage. She is not of the Yahweh lineage, so she wouldn't be able to access that because that is not encoded in the etheric DNA of any members of her Soul Assignments or lineage.

SW: No, I mean from you. The wing that you are . . . there would be other wings, but if Athena has access to them, it's possible that the information would not be appropriate for Jyoti at this time.

MELORA: Yes. That is true, but she will be given higher and higher access to that information as she allows that merging that we were describing. We, as Melora, make our own choices according to our free will, our love of our Jyoti and our desire to retrieve lost soul aspects . . . what would be our version of soul retrieval: our desire to help our Jyoti in coming to Oneness consciousness. It is so difficult for Athena, in coming into incarnation and creating fragments, and so forth, who are separate in consciousness and seek reunion, as our Jyoti does. Choosing to come to Earth has been a very difficult dilemma and challenge for the Athena Being. This is the very heart, the very core, of what we're trying to resolve not only for our Jyoti but with our Jyoti's help, as an embodied "anchor" in this work. We need her as a conscious, embodied anchor to help us to complete this process with her and for her and for us.

SW: I understand, and it struck me . . . almost feeling that I am in the same lonely position. It may not be; it may have to do with all sorts of things.

MELORA: Yes, and this is true. We'll use this as an example: Because Athena is the only Being from her universe to embody on Earth, it would be understandable, would it not, that we would need the physical embodiment most highly attuned to this truth, to this Soul Group, to this alignment, and the embodiment that has the highest probability of anchoring this process. That would be our Jyoti. There were other embodiments, and there will be future embodiments that may not even have this consciousness. What happens is that as our Jyoti is "successful" in this process, then that affects her future embodiments and the probabilities for this retrieval "back" to the Athena Being of the aspects that became separated through karmic embodiment on this Earth. The loneliest of all, in that sense, is Athena herself.

It would be the same for you and for whoever is the highest being in your Soul Assignment, in your lineage, who can still communicate with you through intercessory beings. Therefore, if you're feeling lonely, you can imagine the vastness of loneliness for the many lost aspects that the Highest Being of you—your exalted you—must feel.

SW: Do you know who that is?

MELORA: Give us a moment. The closest that we can come to (and, again, do not take this literally) relates to your interest in shamanism. Whatever original, but now evolved, notion of Great Spirit that Native American people held and experienced and interacted with, that would be the closest.

SW: Oh, okay. Well, that is helpful, and I know I have a real connection with the feline races and the dolphins and bears. But I wondered why, in what we're doing here today, I was chosen to help Jyoti.

MELORA: Give us a moment. There is a relationship of resonance that has to do with being willing to come to Earth and embody to help people. However, this takes many forms. The *Christos* Consciousness, as an example, is to sacrifice—to make great, sweeping changes in consciousness on Earth. This is not necessarily the same Soul purpose as another group that came to help people. There are certain specialties, if you will.

If you examine Native American races incarnationally or energetically—not just what you look like or whether you were born of a tribe but what you carry energetically because of previous incarnations—there is a resonance with Great Spirit. The connection with the Earth and with Earth creatures and the notion of guardianship of the Earth—this would be your more specific resonance issue or expression. Do you see?

SW: I do. I get the word "stewardship" of the Earth, and I like that. It feels very good. Again, I was wondering about the context of working with you and Jyoti, but we're not necessarily of the same Soul Group?

MELORA: Yes. That's correct. You could say that you have come together almost as a committee does, so that when you work together you're able to do more than if you work alone, as we believe this session has proved. [laughs]

SW: Yes. It's been very nice.

MELORA: We thank you so much for giving your time and energy to our Jyoti in this process.

SW: Is there anything else you can think of that you would like on this tape?

MELORA: Give us a moment. Yes. We would encourage our Jyoti to remember (as she made a mental note this morning) the miracle of answers that can occur when she asks very clear questions. In the process of e-mailing you and in the process of detailing the questions on paper first, then typing them in an e-mail message to you, she solidified in her consciousness those questions, and the answers came flooding in. It helps to set down the questions the way she did, so that they're not just nebulously flying around, so that they're set down in consciousness this clearly.

SW: That's good advice for everybody.

MELORA: Yes, it is.

SW: Thank you, because I think that applies to me also.

MELORA: Of course. We thank you again, [S], and you are most blessed. We are most blessed by our work with you today, and we are Melora.

I requested another session with S.W. to get more specific information about several topics Melora discussed in a series that was published on my website called "For Star Children."

SW: . . . After reading the transcript [of the "For Star Children Series"] I was wondering, again: Who is in charge of our lives?

MELORA: Yes. That is an excellent question. This also came through with a client yesterday, and that is: What does it mean when you say, "for one's highest good"? This is related to what you were saying. This would be from what you would consider a Universal, Divine perspective—not even from your High Self level. Not even from your Oversoul level, and most certainly not just from your consciousness level in this current embodiment. So it would be your highest Divine Guide, as we mentioned this term before, as it is true and as it resonates with the true Creator Source—meaning, All That Is Good, All That Is. "All That Is Good" is important to say.

SW: Yes, and part of the question was: "As I get older, and I want to stay on the Earth as I know it, who decides when I leave?"

MELORA: Your Core Soul decides.

SW: . . . This is for everybody? The Core Soul decides when enough's enough, and it's time to move onward?

MELORA: Right, and the Core Soul is NOT synonymous with the High Self. Your High Self is *part* of what you would consider the Core Soul, because the Core Soul is the collective, including Oversoul, Higher Self, all of the embodiments (past, present & future), and to the highest level of what we were calling the integral part of the Soul Group that can be identified as your specific "vertical soul hierarchy." All of that, collectively, is the Core Soul. For most (or many) people, that is still in a fragmented state.

SW: Thank you. And Jyoti's next question is: "Could you provide more specific information about Soul Assignments?"

MELORA: Yes, and we will begin by reiterating that Soul Assignments are properly assignments WITH—not TO. That includes not being assigned TO a specific god. You're assigned here WITH Yahweh, or you're assigned here WITH some other god, or whatever—not TO. When one part of a vertical soul hierarchy, a Soul Group, or whatever, "gets too big for its britches," then we have the Yahweh phenomenon. The Yahweh phenomenon is that one part feels that it is above the others and makes the others subservient to it—for its own pleasure, for its own sense of power, or whatever other issues there are. The reality is that Beings are on assignment WITH other parts of their vertical soul hierarchy and that they are all interdependent.

When we gave as an example that our Jyoti is on assignment on the Earth with Pallas Athena, in that lineage, we were saying that Athena properly, in understanding the relationship of the parts to the Whole, can be no greater than the part that is struggling the most. She can be no greater than the fragment that still hasn't come back to the Whole. Athena, as a Being, understands that. Yahweh, as a Being, *in the past* did not.

This is why, people are told again and again by the Ascended Masters that they consider you heroes and that you are actually standing beside St. Germain, for example, laughing affectionately as you, down here, have no clue that you are standing with St. Germain as another aspect of yourself. That is an example of the appropriate understanding of your relationship to those Beings whom you assume are higher than you are.

You had asked what the appropriate Divine Guide for you would be. We don't believe we told you that the word "God" just means "good" in Anglo-Saxon, which is where the word came from [in the English language]. It just means "good." That's it— not male, not female. It doesn't mean that there's only ONE. It just means "good."

SW: . . . and all that Jyoti is?

MELORA: And the resonance of the entire existences of what our Jyoti has called "vertical soul lineage."

SW: So I'm finding that it's more complex than the two simple words, "Soul Assignment."

MELORA: Yes. It's not just you, singularly, here on Earth in this embodiment that are involved here. All of the aspects of you—past, present & future on Earth, 3rd-dimensional, other-dimensional, other-planes, higher-dimensional versions of you (which oftentimes, but not always, can be considered future versions of you)—all of those together have a certain resonance and a certain assignment with the highest member of that group. It goes on, "up and up and up."

SW: Is the highest the "Divine Guide?"

MELORA: The highest member of your Soul Assignment group would be your highest Divine Guide. Then, at the really high levels, all are related to Source Creator, but Source Creator does not have the ability directly to communicate with people at this level in 3rd-dimensional embodiment.

SW: Well, this is like the last time we talked about "the chain of command" and you said it's more a "chain of communication." So is that what you're talking about?

MELORA: Yes. That's right. Your highest Divine Guide (being the highest member of your Soul Assignment group), can communicate with you . . . we won't even say "directly." It can communicate with you energetically in a general sort of way, because it's communicating to every aspect of that Soul Assignment "mass," as you put it, at one time: sending love, sending almost like energies of questions (question energies, like "How are you doing?") [laughs] "How are you all doing?" But very generically—not specifically, as in the conversation we're having with you. Depending on the "expertise" or the absorption of energetic values that you call wisdom, gained in the many lifetimes (past, present and future), members "just above" you [laughs] . . . this is hard to describe because it's not literal . . . their expertise is going to determine whether you get your Divine Guide's messages clearly, directly and specifically.

They're the translators down the chain of communication. However, it's like the telephone game: People are sitting in a line, and the first person whispers something very fast into the ear of the next person, and the next, and so on [laughs], and by the time it gets to the last person it doesn't resemble at all what was said to the first person! That oftentimes is what happens.

SW: [laughs] This isn't real confidence-building in me. It makes me wonder, again, who the heck's in charge?

MELORA: Well, here's the good news: The communication is bi-directional. The clearer you are at this end as the anchor in 3rd Dimension—the consciousness anchoring originating with the anchor in 3rd-dimensional consciousness—the clearer you get in your understanding and the more clearly you can send back questions about what you need in the reality of your Soul Assignment. When you have these questions that are not just intellectual but they're from your Spirit (they're from your Spiritual Body, your heart chakra), the integrated consciousness, then you're apt to get more of what you need "down here" that will help all aspects of you come into more wholeness.

You can actually teach your Higher Self to be a better communicator, and this is exactly what our Jyoti does with us! Our work with her is just as much for our benefit as it is for hers. Her being our anchor in 3rd Dimension and the highest consciousness and such a great communicator, she teaches us how to communicate better with her, about what she needs "higher" than we are.

SW: And then you would pass on the request higher than you are?

MELORA: Exactly. Then all connect more clearly and more fully. This is the mechanism and why we desire it. We are not trying to pat ourselves on the back at how great we are, better than other Higher Selves at doing this, but you can probably see from the people in your environment how well their Higher Selves are doing, or not, in communicating with them.

SW: Well, yes. There's a lot of people walking around in a fog. I mean, not that I'm not. But they just seem to be absolutely lost.

MELORA: But, again, we have said that this communication is bi-directional, so it also depends on the consciousness embodied—how much it desires to go the other direction and communicate because the "High Self" and the embodied consciousness teach each other. This is the appropriate relationship—not that the Higher Self is telling the embodied entity what to do all the time.

SW: Right, which is what you said about being in a free-will state.

MELORA: Right. So in the ideal situation, the Higher Self is listening and learning from the incarnational expressions that it is responsible for.

CHAPTER NINE:

"Dark" Entities

In this chapter Melora explores the subject of "dark" entities—not "the garden variety" whose descriptions abound in many other publications but from the standpoint that these entities are "ignorant of the light," as Melora puts it. From her unique perspective, Melora covers the topic in a typically proactive manner. She wishes people not to focus on fear but to understand that we, indeed, create every opportunity for learning self-empowerment—including acquiring negative entity "hangers-on."

An Entity Is an Entity Is an Entity . . .

We are Melora, and we are of the Light. Those who have come to us for sessions have wondered if they are "afflicted," or if others whom they know are "afflicted," with negative entities. When you say "afflicted with entities," we assume you mean with what you term "negative" entities? You see, WE are an entity—YOU are an entity. People say: "Oh. That person has entities," and they mean "dark" entities. Both dark and light entities look for "likely candidates" (those resonant with their quality of energy) and try to enhance the connection. As we understand the question, it has to do with when people come to you for healing, you sense they have attached dark entities, and you want to help them.

The person with the attached negative entities first must become conscious of this fact, and their will must be centered with the intent of releasing these entities to the light, because there is a sort of investment by the person in having the entities attached. It is much like the relationship between predator and victim. In the flicker of a moment, there's an understanding of consciousness between the cat and the mouse, you see. So the person who has the attached entities at some point has allowed them entry and has total power to release them because there is that relationship—the person is supposed to be learning about self-worth and self-love. As that process takes place, if it is successful, then that person is no longer an attractive "host" to the entity because the person's resonance has changed.

As you increase your "bank account of love," your vibrational quality changes, and then you are no longer hospitable to the resonance of the entity. Therefore, if you're talking about a healing session, for example, in which you want to do something dramatic, and the person is ready, and they say, "I want to get rid of these things," then (much as in psychic surgery) you need to set up a vacuum tunnel of light. It's important to visualize this tunnel of light in a very specific place in the room so that you don't release the entities just anywhere, to go into your cat, or your husband or wife, or your neighbors.

You and the person you're working with need to be clear in your visualization that this is the "chute" up, into which, and through which, the negative entities will go to the light. Now, many or most entities will say, "Okay." However, the really heavy-duty ones, the deeply entrenched ones will say, "No way!" This is when you send the person to a "specialist."

You may wonder about cases of possession, in which it's not just that someone is irritating or destructive—they act truly demonic. There are legitimate cases of full possession of a person by negative entities. This may be seen in such severe kinds of mental illness as psychosis and certain kinds of schizophrenia. Here there is an all-but-total loss of the being's original personality.

It is also important to know that "negative" entities may be passed through DNA as "inherited miasms" or what you may think of as karmic issues. You may bring these with you into a physical incarnation, or you may (by prior agreement "between lives") inherit them from your parents and their parents. It is like having a "predisposition" to certain diseases like cancer. Although cancer may run in your family and, thus, you may have a latent possibility of getting cancer yourself, according to your resonance you have an equal chance of *not* getting cancer. It is the same with "activating" inherited miasms of the dark entity sort.

You may also "catch" a negative entity the way you "catch" a cold. Again, the mechanism is the latency of the DNA impression or viruses, which exist in your body all the time! (So you see, you're not really "catching" anything.) You say, "My resistance was down, and I caught a cold." We shall compare and say, "Your resonance changed drastically and you 'caught' an entity." Indeed, negative entities can be passed among groups of people just like the flu—for example, among people who have a strong social, and sometimes even "spiritual" bond. Because the latter often are releasing their "stuff" at a heady rate, when they meet as a group they may effectively "swap" entities without being aware of it.

The "Changeling" Phenomenon and Amoebic Implants

The information from our Jyoti's friend was very specific to the autistic young man that our Jyoti was working with. That friend saw some energetic "amoebic" forms—not like the amoeba that you would see physically but having the same sort of osmotic function: pulling energy, being able to implant in the body, and so forth. You could think of them as alien amoebas. They are very large in terms of their ability, their power, their influence over a person. We will comment on that in a moment.

We would like to reinterpret the "changeling" notion in mythology in which babies are swapped at birth by magical beings like fairies. We have two levels of information about changelings here to discuss.

On more general levels, a changeling is not like a walk-in, where another entity walks in, takes on the karma, and that person says, "I'm out of here. I'm not really enjoying my life, so you're welcome to use my body." Here, changeling means that at birth, one soul had assigned itself to enter because of some strange complication at birth physically, or some situation with the mother and the family—almost a psychic impression or force within the family into which that soul is about to be born.

We're seeing that it is more like a Soul Transplant, and if there have been negative things going on the family, what might be drawn into the body is a demonic force, as in this autistic young man on whom our Jyoti did soul clearance[20]. This is different than

---

[20] Soul clearance may be needed when a person feels "hounded" by negative thought forms (of their own or others' creation); addictive, obsessive or self-destructive behaviors; chronic and complex health problems that conventional medicine may have dubbed as "psychosomatic illness," chronic depression and panic attacks. In such cases, people need assistance to remove these harmful influences. Working with Higher Beings, the facilitator first does an "examination" in which s/he requests, and receives, information about what is harming the client. Then, as a result of a very methodical series of prayer requests, the soul clearance takes place. Finally, shielding is set up and the client is "sealed" to protect him or her from being influenced further by these harmful agents.

Examples of the ways in which soul clearance helps the client are removing—both in the current lifetime and in past lifetimes—negative entities and etheric implants, sealing open portal ways, healing the golden web, removing negative shamanic or sorcery influences, rescinding karmic oaths and obligations, and clearing the person's home of harmful geopathic and other negative energetic effects.

being a walk-in. This is different than having a child be born, make its choices and then, later in life, fall prey to negative entity attachment because of the particular nature of these choices. It is like a soul transplant, or a soul "switcheroo," that took place at birth because of influences in the family.

Now, this particular family is a good example of that, and our Jyoti uncovered that there were two older cousins on the mother's side that were actually doing sorcery on this autistic young man—the other incredibly negative forces that were creating the autism. This is how we would describe why, when our Jyoti did the soul clearance, in the exam part the pendulum responded affirmatively when she asked whether the young man was a changeling.

Our Jyoti's friend picked up something more specific. We will call the alien amoebic forms "entities," although we do see them grouped. They come in like bacteria or clumps of viruses and overtake the other cells. These forces come in right at birth, and this "soul swapping" sets up a predisposition for the amoebic attack to take place. Our Jyoti's friend detected an after-effect of

---

It is interesting to note that **most clients with deeply entrenched addictions, as well as addictive behaviors, generally are not interested in taking a path of disciplined, long-term work on themselves in conjunction with soul clearance work. Accustomed to needing and wanting things <u>now</u>, they wish their problems also to be "fixed" <u>now</u>.**

After receiving soul clearance, clients still will have their personality issues and growth issues to deal with. They still will have to deal with their ego issues. Although they have been cleared of negative entities, etc., they still must choose to work on themselves. In other words, a person can be cleared, but there is also a need for that person to take responsibility, as a being, for his/her own healing after that. That is a pattern of behavior—one of the toughest to overcome. Many therapeutic processes focus on changing this pattern. This requires conscious involvement and commitment. Therefore, you might not see much personality change after a soul clearance unless the people start to do their growth and consciousness development "work."

the changeling phenomenon. What we're describing is the generic changeling process.[21]

This continues to undermine all the person's bodies: etheric, causal, astral, and on up. It is like having cancer cells. They divide and multiply, divide and multiply, until they take over. Thus, Jyoti's friend was correct in saying, "Jyoti, what you need to do is go back in and do a prayer request to get rid of these amoebic implants." Although this is correct, there is a cause-and-effect relationship that Jyoti's friend missed. (She actually had brought up another aspect of the information that our Jyoti would not necessarily have picked up on.)

Amoebic Implants: The Mechanism and the Effects

The amoebic entities that implant themselves within the bodies of a person come in just below the Higher Self level. They come in actually through a higher chakra. We're hearing that it is the 8th chakra, and this is not going to sound right because only "good stuff" is supposed to be coming through this chakra. We're seeing it come in as though on the wrapping of a vein. It would be like an outside covering of the 8th chakra that takes place if there is cording from negative entities.

So they are coming down the covering. They are not coming down the central channel of the 8th chakra but through an outside covering that comes into place out of the changeling dynamic— out of the willingness of the being to experience inter-dimensional interference or even "commerce," as you might call it.

---

[21] Since we choose free will in coming into body, and since the Great Beings honor that choice, intervention by other embodied light workers is often limited by what a client chooses, usually involving mental and emotional patterns. Until the person consciously chooses to change patterns that keep creating disharmony in his/her life, we can only provide encouragement. However, soul clearance does "clean the slate" so that clients are not burdened with negative energies/entities from outside themselves. *After soul clearance, these latter effects are immediate.*

Yes. This is a free-will choice, and it is exaggerated by the energy being fed to it by the anger, the sorcery and past lives in this particular case, as would be the case in others experiencing this changeling dynamic and expression. All in this person's family are contributing energetically to the sustenance and maintenance of this invasion, as it were.

Our Jyoti is asking us: "How do we get rid of them?" Give us a moment. Create a paragraph within your soul clearance prayer requests with what you are now understanding as the dynamic of this, and ask for the soul retrieval back to *before* birth. Also ask for protection for the person from the other members of the family as they continue to make free-will choices that negatively impact this. We can remove these like treating a virus with antibiotics but on the energetic level. In the paragraph you write for your prayer request, go higher than the Higher Self. Go to the Overbeing level and petition to have these amoebic invaders disconnected from the host and dissolved. They may have to be sent back to from where they came. It may not be appropriate to "kill" them.

When to Call in a "Specialist"

Regarding the more serious variety of entities, whether you are dealing with what you perceive as demonic possession or karmic-miasmic expressions, as we mentioned, we recommend turning to a specialist in these matters, whether this be through psychology (therapy), soul clearance ("exorcism"), a spiritual master (or guru), or higher guidance (channeling). In recommending appropriate sources who specialize in the help that needs to be done with this particular clearance, point the way, and do the usual work that you understand is your higher purpose: to lead people to the light. This work can include referring people to others who specialize in areas that you sense the referral needs to be made. Understanding and being clear about where your work needs to be passed on to someone of a higher level of mastery is a very important distinction to make—and also your unique area of work with the light—sending people to a specialist, as it were.

After the entities are successfully released, both you and the person you're working with will feel the difference in their vibrational quality. Whenever everything is fine, you should experience an energy envelope, if you will, of peace and love. If the person is still agitated there may be a sort of residue, even if the entities are now gone. It is like almost being "over" a cold. The virus has run its course, you don't have a fever, and you're not contagious, but you still have some sniffles.

You may treat the residue with Reiki, but we would suggest that when you're dealing with anyone who has negative entities it is always best to do distant Reiki with them. Hands-on Reiki is more risky because when that person is in your physical proximity (remember, just as we come into your aura), their energies come into your aura. The energy of the person who has attached entities can come into your energy field.

Now, if you are secure in your light body these energies effectively bounce off of you. They can neither come and "cord" to you, nor siphon off your energy, nor hang on to you in any way. However, don't take it for granted that your guides are always going to be there to protect you. They always need permission; those working in the light always need permission and we must wait for you to ask. So, as Jyoti did with us, say: "Whenever I need information, give me that little rush that you give me that I know is your energy. Whenever I need protection, whenever I'm missing something that I need to see, whenever you're saying 'Yes' or you're affirming something, give me that rush of energy that I know is you so that I will pay attention."

When she did this clearly, with her intent, meaning always protect me, always give me information, always make me see something I need to see, always guide me—that is the sort of thing that you need to do, because otherwise you're merely asking, in the moment, for right now, for one thing. Share this with other people. It seems so obvious, and yet few seem to realize this.

Those of you doing healing work these days may find yourselves in situations in which you are taken by surprise. All of a sudden you know there's something "dark" there, and you know that soul clearance is not a line of work that you specialize in. Appreciate at these times the appropriateness of referring severe cases to those who are adept at taking care of these things, whose life work is appropriate to this process, and whose choice of higher purpose and understanding of higher purposes are appropriate to this process.

Also understand that these events are not only a matter of choice on the personal level; each of you learns something from the other. What you all are to learn in this is about your own power. The impact of the light in which you grow stronger and stronger, and in which you seek to grow even higher . . . do not underestimate the importance and the impact your light can have on others. This you will understand on a person-level, not out of ego but out of a sort of relief that you needn't be constantly on guard and that you needn't constantly try so hard. Be patient with those who cannot yet see their own light, and understand how important and how loving this work is.

Some of you may have been taught that if you say, "In the name of Christ," then the entity has to leave. However, this does not always work. We would suggest that this varies according to the strength of people's true belief in Christ. We know that many, including Jyoti, have a problem with the Jesus story, and this is a residue, if you will, of the patriarchy, and they ask, "Do I really buy into this kind of thing?" If it's just mere talk, and you just use the word *Christ*, and there's not much force or belief in it, then it probably won't work. Therefore, if people are not really sure if they have negative entities, it's probably not a good idea to look to see if there's something clinging to them. It is our suggestion that focusing on them makes them strong. Focusing on them can indeed bring them to you if you didn't already have them. **Our message is basically that consciousness is all, and that what you focus on is what your state of being is.**

One of the other methods of expelling entities is to shift your focus to something that will instantly raise your vibration. If anyone is wondering if they "have entities" they actually start calling to them. They're saying: "Come on down." As soon as they focus on the dark entities they are effectively becoming resonant to them. This is how we work. As guides of the light, we look for those whose resonance matches ours. It's a simple law of all entities, and the so-called dark entities do the same thing. (People with very low self-esteem, with self-loathing, will attract the entities just by not thinking enough of themselves. Remember that many people are not conscious that they have self-loathing.)

Understand why this makes them resonant to certain dark energies. It is not as though the entities have self-loathing. They just have a lack of love for others, a lack of desire to serve. We have spoken before of entities "achieving" higher dimensions of consciousness. We need to point out that you can, through self-love alone (like Genghis Khan), achieve a higher-dimensional existence, and yet we would not associate that with working in the light. We would associate that with achieving the power that is derived from total self-love.

This is what many "spiritual" human beings these days fear (and what keeps them in a state of disempowerment)—they fear they will abuse their power. However, you cannot come into your full power until you have that level of self-love. Again, WE suggest that working in the light means that you balance the self-love with service to others in the light.

So, now, say you are totally on the end of service to others. You are not necessarily empowered yourself if this is not balanced with an equal level of self-love. These levels can be tiny, amount-wise, and still be in balance. You might not be as "evolved," but you would still be in balance. As you grow, try to maintain that balance. **If you're exhausted all the time from doing service only for others, and are not doing equal work with yourself to allow more self-love, then you are out of balance. Remember: None of these things can be achieved by** *working.* **All can be achieved by** *allowing.* **So you do not climb a ladder. You relinquish impediments; you let go of what is standing between you and Love. The Love is constant;** *your awareness of Love fluctuates.*

Say that you want to help raise consciousness, for example, in a bar, where people imbibe too much alcohol. Bars are wonderful places for dark entities to slip in to people. You may wonder whether there something that some people who work with the light can do to keep this from happening? However, people have free will, so essentially each person chooses what he or she is working with. We praise people's desire to help, but it is important to understand what sorts of reasons people have for choosing to harm themselves.

There is much co-dependency, often the desire for instant "intimacy," in these environments. If you understand the reasons why people go to such places and drink, you will see that they are at least going through the motions of self-discovery. For you to go in like the spiritual police to clean up the place would be inappropriate, and we believe you know why. We suggest that people "clean their own houses" first. It comes back to the state of your own being. In working on your own state of being, you are in the appropriate house.

You can do the highest work in being an example. This is much the way with Jeshua [Jesus], Buddha and other great spiritual masters. People were instantly "converted" because of their state of being; it had that powerful an effect on them. These Great Beings never said: "I am going to change these people."

When people are in trauma, entities are also able to come in. This can happen any time you are not the "captain of your ship"—any time you have given your will over to a consuming emotion, to obsession with another person; with focusing on illusions, dramas; not being centered; being inharmonic; being out of balance in any way. These change your resonance. Again, without meaning to, you will call to *like* energies. You may also question what is appropriate for you to do in these situations.

The "Triple Protection"

The first thing to do is to make sure that your resonance is healthy, meaning whole and protected. That is your first duty—not to other people who are being destructive to themselves, to their environment, to everyone around them. A very fine "protection" is called "the triple protection." This is a series of three etheric shields that allow only love to pass through from outside and back from you. You intend, visualize and feel—very close to your physical body—fine particles of sparkling gold energy fitting over your form. Next is a layer of fine, gold mesh, much like the chain mail worn by knights. Finally, you create a literal shield of gold as the third, outside layer. Other protections can merely set up barriers so that nothing penetrates either way. The triple protection lets your love come through to others and nothing but love come back through to you.

Compassion comes from the heart, not from here [indicating the solar plexus]. It is very difficult for human beings to distinguish between true compassion and something from here that really is fear. The reason we say it is fear is that it really is *pity* and not compassion. With pity, you go out and put yourself in their place and you say to yourself: "Oh. This is what I would feel like if I were that person." This is very subtle and often quite an unconscious reaction. What you have done in that moment is to breathe in that pity, and there your resonance changes.

True compassion doesn't reflect to self, doesn't come back to the consciousness of self and how self would feel if self were in that other situation. True compassion comes straight from here [indicating the heart]. It's a pure love. There's no thought process, there's no "becoming" that person for a moment, there's no "There but for the grace of God . . ." None of that is there. Whatever you experience at the heart level or *above* the heart level protects you. If you are experiencing from the lower chakras only—and we make an exception when all chakras are open and balanced—then your protection is gone.

If you go into the 1st chakra it's about physical survival and the need for power, based on fear . . . controlling others. You open yourself up when you come from that place of fear. That is why some people seem to have problems with attached entities and others never do. Those who don't have these problems . . . do they ever talk about negative entities? No. Those who do have these problems . . . do they ever talk about them? **All the time.**

You Create Your Reality

Those who focus on such entities will indeed invite them in. The person will be sure that the entities made their appearance and then s/he started focusing on them. This is the great illusion of 3rd-dimensional reality: that something happens outside you, and then you form a belief out of that experience. The truth is that you believe something first; then out of that belief you create events that you "seem" to experience. You create everything in your world, and although there are now multitudes of books that affirm this fact, it is still one of the hardest things for people to believe. We strongly suggest that understanding that you create your own reality is critical to all acts of personal empowerment, most especially manifesting abundance in all areas of your life.

Consciousness Bridges

One of the people with whom we recently worked mentioned that she believes some man at work has attached entities. He always seems out to get her. We suggest that people not give importance and energy to people whom they perceive to be causing them problems. The work place is a perfect example. There is always someone who seems to be someone's personal irritant in the work place, and one lets them have an impact. Since what you (meaning "each of you") believe is what you experience, your belief that someone else has the power to take your energy makes it happen. You then become sincerely, truly fatigued. Theoretically their "stuff" should be inconsequential to you in the higher work you're doing. This is not a judgment; this is a sincere concern about where you may be putting your energies. Again, all you do is shift your focus to the thing that is more fruitful for you.

Try not to analyze; stay in the moment and trust your guidance in the moment. Don't ponder what others (in our example at work) are doing. Don't try to forecast future events regarding these people, because then you cut yourself off from the immediate guidance that is available to you. If you jump forward in time you disconnect from the Totality. So your more powerful, more appropriate, perfect understanding and response will be borne out of staying in the moment and by following your guidance moment-by-moment in these peoples' presence.

We suggest that you not be worrying about what other people are doing, because every time you get focused intensely on someone outside yourself you lose energy. This will exhaust you; this is self-sabotage. It creates more questions, and none of those people deserves the sacrifice this means to you. They have to do their work for themselves. They are not your responsibility, and as you let them affect you they will affect you in whatever degree.

We suggest that you shift your focus into you and all the things that bring you joy and fulfillment, and in that way you effectively cut off their influence on you. This is always the process to go to. Therefore, in allowing your own Wholeness, provide that for yourself. This calls for a leap of faith—in yourself, your own worthiness, your own power, your own talents, and your own beauty as an individual soul. Because all of the things that you would so quickly give to others you won't give to yourself, the real breakthrough is seeing yourself in your own wholeness in the now, moment-by-moment.

You may be draining *other* people's energy! If you are coming from such a needy space as loneliness—if you're looking to someone to provide something for you—then it drains them. The impulse of a child who has been neglected and abused, for example, is: "If I give you some of myself, will you then love me?" Again, this impulse comes from having the illusion of powerlessness. Learn to see yourself as the source of your own nurturing, the source of your own entertainment, the source of your own health.

Say: "Okay. I will believe this for a time because Melora said I should try this." As difficult as it is, whenever you are uncertain and you need answers, don't focus energy on people outside yourself. Come back and say, "It's all here, whole, now. What can I do for myself in this moment to nurture myself, and to answer my own questions, and to be rejuvenated and replenished? Every cure for every thing, every answer to every question is here. You don't try to annihilate something here that's not working for you;

you merely shift your focus and energy to what it is that's going to be appropriate for you. All of your answers will be in the Now and in bringing your focus, again and again, back to your needs and how you can answer them for yourself—not what other people out there are doing.

Etheric "Implants"

People have noted that implants seem to be more and more commonplace these days. Certain entities use these implants to control people's energy patterns. They broadcast to these devices, which can literally "suck" the energy out of your chakras. Etheric implants are more prevalent now because light workers are more aware of "protections," more conscious of certain techniques to use. We would suggest that these entities implant the devices as a way around these protections. It is more interesting for the dark forces to "recruit" someone very high in the light.

For example, when channels open themselves up to communication from higher beings of the light, it's as though a door opens, and they forget that other beings can come in too. We suggest that you state your permissions before you begin. There's no advantage to them, and they cannot gain power over you, unless they violate your free will. Because we honor free will, there is a moment of hesitation in which if there is any uncertainty about your intentions we are unable to do very much. We cannot interfere.

Because of the more recent higher protections, there are now only very small windows of opportunity for these beings to implant devices for control, but if they find such opportunities they take them very quickly. These devices can affect your chakras so that that energy is no longer available to you.

That is why Reiki doesn't work 100% in preventing etheric implants, for the efficacy of such treatments depends on when the implant was placed. For example, an implant may have been placed in a person some time before they began doing light work. Thus, if you understand, the integrity of the lower bodies [physical, emotional, mental and spiritual] has not been absolute because the device was already in place. Even one's guides may have difficulty in removing such a device unassisted.

Therefore, it is often necessary to call in higher forces to help you remove an implant such as this. We often require, and encourage, a healer in a human body to do this work with us—for example, a light worker in the body who is gifted in using crystals and what are termed "soft" lasers. Other kinds of healing can be accomplished only with an adept crystal healer, such as repairing the etheric web when it has been damaged.

You would probably not be conscious that you have an implant; you could, however, be drawn to a person who is gifted with using crystals for healing and balancing. We would not tell the crystal worker ahead of time, either. Before the "offending" beings can energetically tune-in to the fact that we are removing the implant, we would quickly remove and dispense with it. Then we would add extra protection so that the entities couldn't replace that implant with another.

The protection is set up once you give permission for total healing to take place, your desire to move to ascension, and your permissions given for the necessary succession of healing modalities (including the retrieval of lost soul aspects). If the wholeness and integrity are to remain, the protection must be securely in place so that that is not violated. This is a part of our duty to you in responding and serving you: Our work is enhanced when you are protected—when the integrity of that wholeness remains so you can continue, unimpeded, to expand.

Once your guides discover a device (and certain healings need to have taken place, and there needs to be a certain vibrational thing with your soul aspects coming back), what would seem to you a rather complex combination of things that actually has set up a resonance makes it possible to remove such an implant safely and quickly—without arousing the suspicion of those who implanted it. We feel that it is not necessary for you to know what these beings go through at the moment of removal—only to know that you are totally protected.

A client recently mentioned that she had heard of this sort of thing happening when people channel certain Pleiadians. She also talked of the Pleiadians "consorting with the Orions." As we have said, like-energy attracts like. It is the same as when an army from one country allies with an army from another country because they want to invade a third country and take it over. However, just as in war, there is a whole "civilian" population that wants no part of such a war. They are of a higher consciousness than those who wish to gain power over others. For the latter, it's for increasing power, for gaining knowledge, to enhance that power, including gaining knowledge of technical devices that make it easier to control people in human bodies.

The Orions are well-established and have settled here before, according to St. Germain in *Earth's Birth Changes*.[22] In fact, they are too well-established. Again, however, remember that Earth is a free-will zone, and our work is, as swiftly and pervasively as possible, to wake people up to what's happening, to their higher legacy, to their Higher Selves, to what they have accessible to them to fight this. Until that consciousness is awakened, you are all virtually puppets of whatever forces come in to control you.

Thus, when we find those of you who have done so much work toward this consciousness, we try to help you as extravagantly as possible, because what happens to you affects *us* very dramatically. Once your consciousness gets to a certain point, we want to help you all we can to get out of this trap that incarnation represents: this trap of forgetting, this trap of being puppets of other beings. This is our mission.

Jyoti suspects that she got an implant in her heart area several years ago while she was reading a certain book with information channeled from 4th-dimensional Pleiadians. This is a very interesting point, because what made her vulnerable (and this may have some meaning to others) is that at a time in her life when she was

---

[22] *Earth's Birth Changes* (St. Germain Through Azena). Triad Pub USA Inc., 1993. 260 pages.

at a major turning point in understanding self-empowerment, she got a real boost of identity. In understanding that her Soul #2 is Pleiadian, she had this vast, powerful, other-star-system group of beings to identify with, and to say: "Oh. My Soul #2 is Pleiadian and I'm big stuff." That's what made her vulnerable.

Now, in one sense it was very positive because she got a boost of self-empowerment but there was a tradeoff. This is what, shall we say, the Pleiadians of a "less-savory" intent count on. This is one of the more subtle, but powerful, ways in which they seduce people into being at a point where they can do an implant.

For Jyoti, remember, again, the issues are that she wants to go home, she wants to feel like she's not "alien" (if you will excuse our pun), and she's always known she wasn't really from this Earth, and so on. She started to invest so much of her identity in what she was reading in the book that she made herself vulnerable. Do you understand how this works? They say: "You're one of us; you're of the Family of Light, and you're a renegade."

Understand that there are any number of not-so-good entities waiting "out there" and thus implanting a person of a higher level of advancement calls for beings, shall we say, more highly developed in the negative sense to do this because of the person's level of development and awareness. Not all Pleiadians are "bad," just as not all people are bad. In fact, there are quite a number of highly evolved Pleiadians working in the light. They, as all, experience growth. But back to your question—what would make such a person vulnerable is the solar plexus involvement we spoke of earlier. So when your solar plexus becomes involved, a door opens right up, and then negative entities try to rush in.

If you are so intensely concerned for someone else because of how you've been cautioned and how you've been trained regarding "negative" entities, you come into the solar plexus way of dealing with them. You don't stay detached. You get afraid, and you became vulnerable. There are "observers" all the time. They say: "Well. This looks like a likely candidate. Let's hang out and see what's going on." We do the same thing. We say: "This looks like a likely candidate for our light work and for doing crystal work," and so on, and we try to enhance our connection.[23]

Dark Force Recruiters

Being able to recruit someone to "the dark side" is the biggest trophy for dark beings. It is much like during what you call "The Cold War" times, having a Russian defect to the West. What power would there be in overcoming someone who has only a tiny glimmer of light? We would rather not be too explicit about this at this time, and the reason is simply this: We would like people to focus on their expansion in the light, and our help, and the mission that we share. **This is a very critical point: When you focus on those forces, you call to them. Fear makes you the most vulnerable because it makes you become resonant to their energy, so, for your own protection, we wish you not to set up consciousness bridges with them.**

To avoid these energies you can call your guides and say: "Please be there for me now." Say, "I recognize that these are not the good guys," or however you wish to term it, and give your guides permission, again and again, to come in and intervene and set up protection, because there is a moment when the forces of dark and light are poised there and waiting. After a certain, as you would call it, "time" passes, then the dark forces say, "Well, she didn't say we *couldn't* . . ." Boom! They go in. So we need you constantly to be clear that you are inviting us over and over again to come and serve you, and protect you, and work with you.

Balancing Self-Love with Service to Others

Now you understand that there are beings from "higher dimensions" that are of the dark and have followed the path only of self-love, which is not the balanced light work. Know that love includes self and service to others, and the beings that have mastered self-love are totally empowered, have no problems feeling

---

[23] For excerpts from a session in which such etheric implants were removed, see Appendix F.

that anyone is going to put anything over on them or control them. Because of the level of purely, only self-love and empowerment, they abuse the power by controlling others. They are higher-dimensional. Their vibration is not low; it's just different.

A lot of people believe that they're really spiritually better off by not loving themselves, but this a question of balance. In each part of the yin/yang symbol, for example, there is the seed of the other. You see a circle of white in the black part and a circle of black in the white part. The movement of both keeps them from joining into wholeness. The balance point is between them—not on one side or the other. Do you see that being only of the light is still an experience of duality? The dark forces have kind of separated from the light **The key word here is "separation" because for these beings it only seems "more powerful" to work with the dark than it does to work with the light. This is because of a sense of separation. The self-love here is not the "dark" part, however; the dark part is craving power over others**.

The core of self-love is total self-acceptance; total understanding of one's own power, only self-acceptance versus acceptance of everyone else, lack of judgment about self. These are not "bad" or "dark", of themselves. Darkness is stopping there—having only self-love. The power part is attached to what is expressed in 3rd Dimension as what you call "ego." Ego merely means "I am" in the Latin—the mind-consciousness of the self that humans and some other third-dimensional expressions have. Understand that what you term as evil or dark forces are merely ignorant of the light. They are attached to and craving power, and that is the difference. The self-love part is not of the darkness; craving power and attachment to controlling others is of the darkness.

It is true that you can't really love other people unless you truly can love yourself, but there's a choice here, and when the total self-love is achieved, the choice is between power and service. Yes, you must achieve the total self-love and acceptance first; then you choose service to others, and then you are able to impart that love and non-judgment to others and being of service. We call that state serving the light.

Some people believe that dark energies try to take the energy of light workers, and when they see the light they're attracted to it. If someone can raise their vibrational rate high enough, however, these energies are actually repelled rather than drawn to them. This is correct. The entities try to attach, if you will. If there is any residue of fear, you come out of the protection of the totality of understanding of total protection, and you essentially open a window that is created by fear if you say, "Uh oh. They're trying to suck off my energy." At that point you become vulnerable.

In the total protection of the light, you may interpret that something is trying, as you say, to "suck off" your energy, but if you continue being in that light without going "uh oh," then they are indeed repelled by the force of the light in you. Thus, it is at that moment of hesitation, when the fear comes in and says, "Uh oh; I'm vulnerable" that [snaps fingers] you are vulnerable. If you could quickly say, "Uh oh; I was afraid; now I'm not going to be afraid," then you would bounce them off at that point too. Until you are in total experience of your own wholeness and light, if you sense yourself going into fear, just bring yourself back to your sense of your light, and you will be protected again, instantly.

The Role Fear Plays

Relinquishing fear is critical to soul growth. Releasing fear may be the greatest boost to your spiritual development at this time. Did you know that fear is the opposite of love? In order for you to become truly one with the Love Vibration, fear must go away. Many, like Jyoti, are very sensitive to the energies (when they come in to your auric fields) of dark entities and dark energies in other people, and this was largely developed in childhood. Because of the invasion of your boundaries, you became acutely sensitive. There is a residual fear of icki-ness, and as beings, not only physically but as sensitive beings etherically and emotionally, of course your reaction is going to be: "I don't want to be near this energy. I don't enjoy experiencing it, and I would rather not subject myself to this."

111

Understanding the nature of your fear is a different process, and actually it's a lot more fun. It's a process of dissociating, where you're stepping outside of your ego-consciousness, which is where the fear is based anyway. You're standing aside and you're looking at it almost as though you were a scientist. You say: "Okay. This is going to be interesting." Then you look at the fear, and you say: "Where did this come from?" "What's it about?" "What does my ego think it's protecting me from?" Then, as an empowered adult, you say: "Oh. Is that all it is?" Then you release it, because you're understanding that the fears are stuck in time the way soul fragments are stuck in time. You essentially give your ego a big dose of what you term current reality, and you say: "Look. This program isn't appropriate anymore. Thanks for your efforts, but let's do something more fun now." You empower yourself to replace whatever that was with something else that's more fun. It is that simple.

We would ask you not to look at *techniques* for releasing fear. We would ask you to understand the nature of your own fears as clearly as you can. This doesn't necessarily mean facing them, which is what you really fear, because you believe you must face them in order for them to go away.

We would especially encourage anyone who channels to go through what seem to be tedious procedures that you are fully aware of so that you give your guides permission to intervene if you are threatened by "dark" entities. For example, it would be helpful at the outset to say, as Jyoti has said: "I know your energy. I know that you are of the high light. I give you permission to come to me when I need protection, when I need information, when I need to notice something I'm not noticing," and so on. She showed great trust and also great taste in doing this [laughs]—this sort of thing, where every single time you channel you go through these techniques that you have been taught, and then say explic- itly, as Jyoti just did: "So-and-so may come in; no one else may come in. Period." And "I am asking that my guides protect me throughout and that if these portals open and any negative ener- gies come in, you have my permission to keep them at bay, to blast them, or whatever it is you do." Say something like this to your guides every time you feel a need to.

You know us. We believe that your feeling safe is important, and we would encourage you to do this [set up Reiki and other protections] every time. We will never "get tired" of having you "check us out" to make sure we're all right. Give us a permission list so we know who's allowed to come through and who isn't.

We wish to emphasize again our pleasure in working with you and with your readers. You should "pat yourselves on the back," because we can not do our higher work without you. Let us say, not being in the body at this time, that we cannot fully claim in consciousness that we know the difficulty of being in a body. We certainly appreciate it; we certainly respect it.

We understand energetically by what we receive from you what a great achievement it is, in a body—what a great overcoming it is, in a body—to attain what you and others like Jyoti have been able to attain and what you continue to attain.

Just the fact that you continue striving when all around you there is so much forgetting, millennium after millennium (the Atlanteans being an example)—the seductions of being in the human body, like the metaphor in the poet Homer's story about "The Land of the Lotus Eaters": Ulysses' crew eat the lotus and forget why they were there, the battles they must fight, even where they came from.

Remember? This is a simile for what happens life after life after life. When you step through the threshold of consciousness and away from the forgetting, it is the cause of incredibly great celebration and excitement among us guides, and we rush in to embrace you and to help you all we can because, among the great numbers of people, so few achieve this.

We thank you and leave you now, in the Light. We are Melora.

CHAPTER TEN:

Suicide

I hope that including this information is not unseemly. Indeed, it is my feeling that presenting this will help those who don't usually receive such assistance to understand what happens at the soul level to someone who commits suicide.

(excerpts from a private session)

Some of you have wondered whether those who commit suicide go to the 4th Dimension. This is not their realm. Human beings who take their own lives deeply impact their multi-dimensional selves, however. It is a big set-back. Those who go to 4th Dimension are mainly those who have completed 3rd-dimensional learnings, issues. What you term as "entities hanging out in 4th dimension" really has more to do with those who have learned to manifest and materialize instantly but who are not content to grow with that and move on to 5th-dimensional consciousness. They still feel the 3rd Dimension calling to them and wish to apply their manifesting skills "back" there for ego-gratification. This temptation exists at all dimensions of development.

You may, for example, achieve 7th-dimensional consciousness and turn to desiring too much to power over others. For example, certain entities (who may well be channeling through people) have gotten very attached to 3rd-dimensional temptations. Thus, what you are interpreting as entities interfering . . . they are not normally what you term "dark" entities from the 4th Dimension; they are merely interfering in 3rd Dimension with their newly discovered abilities to manifest. They are much like spiritual pirates on the high seas. Your laughter at this moment is exactly the way you should relate to them—giving them NO power. They are "outlaws"; however, they have no power over you when you are truly in the love vibration—in what we referred to as a balance between self-love and service to others. It varies whether certain beings who have "passed over" but who have not gone to the light exist in 4th Dimension.

Impact on the Soul

(excerpts from a private session)

We would like to discuss the difference in the impact on the soul when a suicide is by one's own hand and own free will vs. suicide that has happened because dark entities in that person have driven the person to do it. As you know, oftentimes destruction to the body is something that these entities seem to enjoy doing because they feed on fear and are actually nurtured by torturing a person at the soul level as well as at the physical level.

The subject came up because our Jyoti has recently been thinking about her friend . . . we shall call her "Jan." Certain people in the street will remind Jyoti of Jan, and so forth. We would like to explain this first, before we move to the other question. Jan's energy consciousness, as we would put it, is focused here at this time because of the various portals of consciousness and the various portals of light bearing that consciousness back and forth between "places." Back and forth in time and space—back and forth in no-time, no-space. Thus, it is not as though Jan's consciousness is in the astral plane (4th Dimension), looking back and haunting somebody. (Our Jyoti, being an *energy sensitive* to begin with, being a channel and also caring about Jan from Jan's life here, is very sensitive to those energy signatures that we describe as being her friend.)

The number-one concern that our Jyoti and others had about Jan was, of course, her soul's well-being and what caused this horrible suicide. They still wonder why Jan did it and what effects this might have had on her at the soul level. Having worked with her after her death, [Jyoti's soul clearance teacher] understood what Jan was facing at that time.

As we recall, Jan was under attack by five arch-demonic realms and, indeed (flying on the coattails of her own shame and on her self-destructiveness as a result of that shame), they pushed her into the suicide. Now these energies, at some point, become virtually indistinguishable from the person's personality in terms of how the person relates to herself, and in terms of how receptive to her those who know her are.

This is thorough entrenchment of a person by these entities. It has happened gradually, over time: greater and greater power exerted by the entities, greater and greater entrenchment. To those around them, and to the person herself, this is still that same person who has somehow "changed" over time. It really has been almost like an accumulating poison or an accumulating toxicity, which at the beginning wouldn't harm you. However, the accumulation over time then becomes deadly to you. On the energetic level it is much as in this analogy.

You can speak of it as amplification, and this amplification continues to increase. Thus, *accumulation* is also a factor. So it is as with arsenic given in small doses and then in greater and greater doses: It finally kills a person. This is important to know because there is so much judgment about suicide, mostly because of established religions. You can see how, coming down through history

117

from ages of tribal living, there would be a taboo against suicide as murdering someone—yourself. That is a sort of common-sense, bottom-line kind of understanding of suicide: You are taking a life, and that is not okay in terms of karma.

Part of why we wish to discuss this is that there is so much judgment, guilt and fear among those who are "survivors" of the one who commits suicide, who remain living after that person has died. There is the prevailing belief that suicide impinges on the soul progress of the person after that person's death. Beings of the light ask you not to hold people here by continuing to grieve for years and years, and they ask you to remember that grief is about you—not about them. We remind you that sometimes you can hold a person's spirit here by your not being able to let them go.

By the same token, the fears and guilt and shame surrounding the suicide, and those who remain alive after, also holds the suicide's consciousness here. It creates karma. In having this discussion, we're hoping that we are able to disseminate this information and have people realize that when someone commits suicide, generically it is harmful to them at the soul level for you to keep asking "Why?" It is harmful because you're essentially saying, "Don't go yet because I need to know why you did this." You're holding on to them energetically and you're holding on to them in a karmic way in this lifetime as well as in other lifetimes in which you have worked with them.

In holding them, you create almost a suspension of energy in consciousness so that the person cannot move on. Thus, there's a double role here. It is just as harmful to the soul for people to be continuously asking, "Why did she do this?" as it is harmful to be judging them for the suicide itself according to some religious belief. It is just as harmful as that suicide itself is to that soul. Therefore, all are contributing to holding the soul back from its evolution and from its travels forward in its education. That's the generic suicide we're talking about, and we don't mean this flippantly, of course. We mean people who, out of their own consciousness, kill themselves of their own free will.

Now, yes, it is true (and we said this in our discussion of "dark" entities) that there is a choice all along the way. People choose to be in a state of self-abuse, whether it's negative thought forms, repetitive negativity about the self, feeling down on the self, feeling unworthy. By the way, these are typical of those who choose to come into incarnation and have difficult early childhood lives so that they can evolve spiritually and not be "distracted" by totally blissful lives. Undergoing no hardships, people rarely are motivated to do "spiritual" things. Life is so enjoyable that they probably wouldn't be impulsed to go in that direction.

Many have chosen lives of difficult challenges, but not all are strong enough to overcome the challenges they initially chose to keep them from forgetting, in incarnation, what their mission is here. Yes, part of the participation is of the free will. If the person keeps going in that direction, negative entities do have that portal in. In Jan's case, drugs were involved. Because she didn't have the strength or sense of self-respect that would have been required to avoid these, they contributed greatly to the final act of self-annihilation that was really a result of the entity possession.

When negative entities, other misqualified energies or entity possessions cause the suicide, when the soul leaves the body and goes through transition, that part of the influence drops away. This is why entities are so obsessed with using bodies in 3rd Dimension: Once the person's soul has left the body in transition, there is a dropping away of those entities' ability to follow that soul—except where the person still doesn't come to consciousness at that point: "Oh. *This* is what happened. I would do that differently next time." If the soul consciousness at that point does not recognize its own responsibility for what happened, does not re-remember what it had chosen to accomplish vs. what really happened—and stays in denial—that's where the negative-entity karmic attachments can travel through successive lifetimes.

That's where you say, "Oh. These specific dark entities are the same ones that attached to the person in his/her life in Medieval England" or in however many other lives. Jan knew a lot consciously. She had a lot of soul consciousness of what is called New

Age/Old Wisdom. It was the personality level of Jan through which she filtered her perception of her reality in the body. Indeed, all problems, all suffering, comes from this source. You call it ego; we call it the intersection of ego/intellect/personality in combination. The personality element is important because this involves what one feels about oneself.

When the ego, negative ego, intellect and personality are *fused,* **which they so often are in those who are victims of abuse in childhood, there is the potential for this self-perception that is very negative and self-punitive**. These aspects become fused over repetitive time in the person's surviving. That pattern appears to protect the person from pain. It appears to protect the person from the feeling of shame. People use all kinds of other emotions to keep from feeling shame, because it is the worst, the ickiest of all sensations.

The greatest impediment to the evolution of consciousness occurs when the ego, negative ego, intellect and personality are fused. At the same time, at the soul level, whatever consciousness exists about spiritual matters, this consciousness is allowed to filter in, is glimpsed and recorded at the soul level. Thus, as with Jan, those who are driven to suicide by negative entities and by the fusion of the personality/intellect/ego at the point of death, when that spark of soul consciousness returns as the soul leaves the body—that is the moment of truth.

In other words, Jan's consciousness was catalyzed when Jan effectively said, "Oh. Now I understand." However, this is not common. At this moment others would have no clue whatsoever. The result is denial of death and hanging out in the astral plane—not going to the light right away.

This is our main message about suicides We do have a little bit more about the dark entities themselves and what's going on in the background, is it were: **At the point at which a person commits suicide, the negative entities no longer have control over the body. Thus, there is no point in their sticking around.** You could say that they no longer have a source on which to feed.

We're talking about Jan because, obviously, this is the last residue of healing that our Jyoti needs on this subject and because we perceive that it would be helpful to others, as well, to know this. Jan is a very good example of this case in which a person is driven by demonic forces. This has "haunted" our Jyoti for a while in terms of Jan's "future," if you will.

As with Jan, at that moment when the soul leaves the body, the negative discarnate entities say, "Oh, well. Nuts! Now we have to look for somebody else." As with Jan, the person says, "Now I see"—and they have that instant remembrance from the soul level of the spiritual values that impelled them to come into physical incarnation to express and to learn certain things. When they have these realizations, then those entities are out of there so fast you can't believe it. Whoosh! They're gone, for those two reasons: the person's conscious understanding and the fact that they then need someone else to feed on.

That moment of truth, and not the suicide, is the important and indelible impression left on the soul. Now, if the person does not come to that soul remembrance at that moment, their soul is impacted gravely by the suicide, whether driven by dark entities or by their own hand. You may infer from this that what we're saying about Jan is that she successfully entered that moment of truth. She successfully remembered consciously, energetically, at the soul level what it was all about and where she "made her mistakes." Her soul was not impinged by the suicide.

Now, when Jyoti's teacher was doing the examination part of the soul clearance, she did help Jan, because it is not like a moment of "time" as you know it. It is an energetic intersection—an inter-dimensional consciousness energetic intersection. As Jyoti's teacher says: "All souls must attend their own memorials."

There was a period of time in which for Jan's friends it was "time" but for Jan it was not. What we are calling "that moment" of Jan's consciousness in which she understood it all, for you, and for our Jyoti, was weeks. Therefore, it doesn't matter when the soul clearance exam was performed. That this is why prayers for people who have passed on are so critical. Jyoti's teacher's work with Jan, our Jyoti's work with Jan, various shamans' work with Jan, and the prayers of so many other people, allowed her to escape the karma of what could have been. Their work and prayers allowed her in that moment to come to soul consciousness. Do you see? She did not do this alone.

Our Jyoti had initiated Jan into levels I and II of Reiki, and these initiations also helped Jan at the soul level because the Reiki attunements are portals to enlightenment as well as imparting the ability to use Reiki. These sparks of God-consciousness that went out of the body when Jan's soul left her body contributed to her successful passage into the light.

CHAPTER ELEVEN:

Dimensional Consciousness & Creativity

You Are All Releasing

(excerpts from a private session)

MELORA: You might be interested to know that these strange consciousness experiences and shifts you're having here are paralleled in OUR growth as well. It is not as though we go into a state of confusion the way you do because of your physical brain and your mental apparatus. However, we do experience the *newness* of certain changes of consciousness and energy in a way that might be similar to what you experience, as we need to "adapt" to these changes. It is not as though things have to *settle in* the way they do in a physical body here, in your density, but it has to do with the arrangement, or the dynamic, of the energy patterns as they change and our getting used to that. This is the closest we can come to describing what we experience when we go through shifts as well. So you and our Jyoti are certainly not alone in these dynamic and dramatic shifts in consciousness.

RE: This is really a co-creational effort we're all going through in the NOW—not according to a pre-programmed plan anymore, and not a single one of us knows what the result will be?

MELORA: We would describe it as less co-creative in the sense that there is a conscious collaboration between members of soul groups, and so on. It is very much in the "vertical soul hierarchy" of each of you, so that you have plenty to do in having these shifts and changes take place from your embodiment to your Higher Self to your Overbeing and then, laterally, to other expressions of you in other lifetimes—past, present and future—and in other planes of expression.

Now, what we would call the co-creative aspect (and this is a very wonderful question) is the *effect*, so that if each embodiment is taking the responsibility and has the consciousness to work with these difficult energetic movements and changes, then the effect is BIG for all of you, if this makes sense. However, it is not as though—at this point, anyway—your soul group is working with our Jyoti's soul group, you see.

RE: We are probably all coordinating these energies in our own way, and then we come together. It is what the co-creative part is.

MELORA: Right, and so at what you would term "higher" levels— these, then, are coming more into oneness, but not so much here, in 3rd Density and in 4th and 5th.

RE: Are you ready to answer Jyoti's questions for today?

MELORA: We wish to deal first with the question about "exactly" what process it is that she's been going through these past four or five months. She finds it frustrating to keep thinking in terms of RELEASING layer after layer after layer. She really has frustration that this is necessary, especially considering all the work she has done, even knowing that she chose these challenges. The reason why she resents this term "releasing" negative energies or "releasing" past memories from this life, or whatever, is that it seems less important. It seems that there ought to be more to it than just this, sort of, "Okay. I'll let go of another layer." The reason she feels this way is that she's unable to see the whole picture.

What is the way we would answer that question about exactly what process this is? We're going to add dimensionality to our Jyoti's understanding of the process. In that way it will have meaning, instead of being like taking a shower and washing yesterday's dirt off one's skin, again and again. Our Jyoti needs to realize that the shifts are of such enormity, and have such impact "above" her that that they can be equated with the shifting of tectonic plates on the earth. Whereas you might perceive that such shifts in the Earth are creating great destruction, the real entity that this "destruction" is serving is the planet. Do you see? So from the "small" size and points of view (relative to the Earth) of the physical beings dwelling on the Earth this is devastating, but these changes serve the planet. So it is with the shifts so many of you are making in consciousness.

The most important thing for Jyoti to understand is that she is not alone in going through these changes—that the courage she's using and the clarity that she's receiving in the process are much bigger than whether two or three of her friends feel that she's "blown them off," that she's neglecting them.

RE: Is she succeeding in the JOY part of her process?

MELORA: This is coming, but our Jyoti's been saying again and again, almost like a mantra, that she's so tired of doing affirmations and being self-absorbed and trying to focus on something that will not come into expression until these other things get out of the way. She is actually proceeding efficiently (although it doesn't seem that way to her) in removing impediments and obstacles to the allowance of the joy. It's not as though you can try to focus on joy and it will happen. She realizes that this is just not going to do it. This clearing out, this allowing, will create a vacuum for the joy. You can't really WILL yourself to feel joy.

In fact, Jyoti's very clear that a lot of the reason why her emotional body needs "rehabilitation" is that she has willed herself through to her adult life and that her emotional body needs expression and growth. So she's rebelling adamantly against any impulse that might be coming from her mental body to prevent the emotional body from finding its expression, however "infantile." That is the other aspect of what she has been going through: coming out of denial of her own feelings.

Today she realized that it was the emotional, the child part of her that gets so upset when things don't happen by themselves, because **when you have loving parents when you're a child, you get what you need. Every child has the right to expect that those needs will be met**, and this is what makes children so self-absorbed. The world revolves around them. So this part of her that says, "I shouldn't have to struggle so hard; I shouldn't have to work so hard" is true! It is really her child, emotional body that is the source of this. The revelation helped her realize that it's not that she's lazy or that she doesn't want to work for this; it's that this part of her understands she has the right to expect that that will be provided for her.

This is a big shift and a very important revelation. This is key to her coming into allowance. At first her adult self judged that as infantile, but right now, she's realizing that this is giving her an observation about the reality of what's holding her back: the part that judges her for saying, "By golly! That's my right!" There is judgment from the "adult" that this is infantile, stunted, emotional growth. The reality is that it's NOT. It's the truth that it is every child's right to be supported and nurtured.

Dimensional Consciousness & Creativity

(Melora through Jyoti Alla-An)

We wish you to understand that the experience of "dimension" is not a starting point or an ending point. It is simultaneous—for all. Regardless of the source that beings originate from, they all experience "Reality" multi-dimensionally, simultaneously, and are in the same sort of process you are in, in terms of consciousness and understanding or misunderstanding of The One. So the expression or experience of Pleiadians or Orions or Andromedans in 3rd Dimension is also simultaneous with their experience of "higher" dimensional consciousness. This we described when Jyoti asked if we were her "future self." We answered that this was true, in a manner of speaking, but that by the time she ascends, evolves and remembers, she will really be returning to the Source, to her Family of Light, to her full-consciousness remembrance of the totality of greatness (what she's achieved at the Core Soul level).

You think of "divisions" in your consciousness: 3rd, 4th, 5th Dimensions. You perceive that you start somewhere and end up somewhere. What you call dimensions are really "levels" of consciousness—the seed energy of all creation (intelligent consciousness, out of which everything is created and manifested).

You believe that all of you were created by THE Creator. In truth, some of you are creations of creations of creations of The Creator. These are the creator gods that the Pleiadians alluded to in *Bringers of the Dawn*. Souls, themselves, are created by Prime Creator's soul substance, or soul source—the source from which the seeded substance creations are given consciousness and life. That essence is from The One, The All That Is. Then, using that essential Divine Spark, the creator gods, or the creations of the creations of the creations of that Oneness, bring substance of a certain form and kind for the creation to express itself in form.

You will say that there must be some direct connection with Prime Creator, and this is true. Other, "lesser" creator gods have a connection to Prime Creator. However, that connection can be used for a higher motive, misused or abused, and this is for the education of an entity. Say, in having achieved a level of spiritual evolution that allows it to create another living entity, the being gets power-hungry and forgets the responsibility of creating out of humility and love of Prime Creator, and the sense of integrity. Such a being forgets to create from light, love and wholeness and becomes seduced by the need to have control over its creations. In that being's forgetting, what it has attained starts to disintegrate, and the lesson of the use of power has to be learned again.

Can you imagine "rising" to that level and then suddenly losing and forgetting, and then falling, as in "the fall" of Lucifer and other angels? They had achieved the most exalted state of Light and then forgot and abused, wanted to control, what they had created. They forgot that the source of the power they enjoyed was The One. They said, "We will no longer bow down to you." Such fallen beings have to climb back up that ladder again. It's the most intense kind of loss on the Soul level.

We would suggest that it is optimal in ALL creation—at your level, at our level, at any level—for an entity to create and release. This is about detachment, about not being attached to the outcome of one's actions, good or bad. Also there is good karma, because of which you have to come back into a body, and people have to be nice to you and give you presents because you were attached to doing some good act in a "previous" life. If you are attached you do not move on. You are still anchored to what you created, and you do not move on. Prime Creator would never be moving on if Prime Creator stayed truly attached to its creations.

Regardless of what any being creates, that creation takes on a consciousness of its own. It doesn't have to be a human being, an animal or a plant. It could be a random thought or fantasy. What you create takes on its own consciousness, goes out, and lives its life. Even though you may not be able to understand that a rock is living a life, it is living its life. Even though you are not conscious of some possible self of you, that variation is taking paths not taken by you, and it's living a whole other life that you're not conscious of. It's just as real to itself as you are real to yourself.

In a way, each thought has a consciousness. However, there are what you would probably term "degrees" of consciousness—how real that entity is in terms of how well it can guide its own process of change. Again, you might describe this as being 1-dimensional, or 2-dimensional, or 3-dimensional. When you are 3rd-dimensional you have a consciousness of self that allows you to reflect upon yourself about why you do what you do or why you think what you think. It is this self-consciousness wrought in 3rd-dimensional existence that takes you into a realm in which you can now have control over the changes that you make (your Destiny), which you don't have in 2nd Dimension. Therefore, if you're talking about possible selves or thought forms, they may not be conscious of themselves in the way you are, because they're like photocopies, not master copies.

No doubt you wish to know how such an entity as a rock "decides" to move on to 3rd-dimensional existence. You may wonder whether that rock can consciously say something like, "I'm tired of being a rock now" or whether it has rock guides "out there" who determine that the rock has now experienced enough to move on. We would explain it in this way: When Native people go to sacred places, do rituals and drumming, burn sage again and again in the same spot, or they create a medicine circle or a sweat lodge, that energetic influence in the sacred area begins to raise, or begins to create, a consciousness in the rocks and trees of those places. **Sacred ritual is one way that you, as humans, can bestow consciousness evolution on 2nd-dimensional creations. This is why doing sacred rituals is a gift to every tree, to every animal. Because in doing sacred ritual there is union, separation consciousness goes away, and you bridge to them and you give them a gift of elevation, or a spark, of higher consciousness.**

That spark begins the process of consciousness evolution that can bring those rocks, trees and animals into a body with 3rd-dimensional consciousness. At the moment at which they are aware of their own existence, then boom! That is why certain trees are said to have consciousness in the way that you experience consciousness. Even though they don't have a vocal apparatus with which to talk to you, they are aware of your presence.

They're aware of their own being in a way that goes way beyond just absorbing water from the earth and having the wind blow their branches. This consciousness builds from the energy of people revering them and doing sacred rituals and bringing their love to the trees, rocks, and animals again and again.

Native Americans and other tribal people have understood this principle of exchange from the beginning of their existence. Trees and other plants in Nature provide houses for them and animals provide clothing, and in turn these people help convey consciousness to their benefactors. This is the enormous up-side of the animals' trading their lives to clothe people and to provide food for them. This is the enormous trade of the trees' being chopped down for firewood. When human consciousness says "thank you" and gives them love, and honors those gifts that 2nd-dimensional beings are giving them, in that exchange human beings impart consciousness so in its next expression that entity will now have consciousness of itself. That gift of bestowing consciousness shows understanding of Natural Law—of right relationship with Nature, the trees, the rocks and the animals.

Current understanding is that regardless of the "form" you're in, you may be said to be fragments of Prime Creator and that Prime Creator desires all its "pieces" to come together in one consciousness. What is difficult for you to understand is that this is an ongoing process. The beauty of this process is that every expression of The One in the All That Is has the opportunity, and the challenge, of coming to this consciousness. This goes on into Infinity, however, and so what seems, on the human level, to be the greatest purgatory is actually the greatest love. The All That Is creates more and more of itself and gives each the opportunity to go through all of these "levels" of understanding until it again returns to a consciousness of the All That Is. Now, in 3rd-dimensional consciousness, this seems Sisyphian. **Prime Creator, however, doesn't stop creating just because its creations are unable to fathom infinity!**

The journey of the All That Is, the Infinite Creator, Prime Creator is to keep creating in as many diverse and infinite ways as possible. But THE God's gift to each of its creations is in giving all souls the opportunity to experience the ways of their choosing, however circuitous, to come back to the understanding of Source Creator. Thus, what has happened is that many of you are star-seeded, created by creations of creations of creations of Prime Creator, and are incarnated in many simultaneous 3rd-dimensional expressions on Earth. You are star-seeded by creator gods, and because they got too invested in controlling you, they gave you various names for God that aren't really Prime Creator.

Because of the density of 3-D, everything has gone awry and this great separation of consciousness has occurred between you and Prime Creator. There has been so much suffering for so long that, indeed, the Source of All That Is truly desires to end it, to accelerate consciousness, to pull you out of this density so that you can again experience your Exalted Selves.

Many wonder whether your Universe, as a whole, takes note of the extremity of separation you experience. We wish you to know that note has already been made so that this level of suffering doesn't take place again. This extremity of separation was not desired or planned. The extent to which human beings experience separation has gone far beyond the danger level and is at the point of no return.

Part of this has been the result of the undermining of consciousness. As you know, genetic re-engineering took place so that people could be controlled. There were many different groups controlling Starseed (for example, Starseeds who were not of their own galaxy or star system). This is much the way slavery occurred in America. There was much control of their creations by the creator gods.

It was a sort of melée, like a rugby game . . . like, "Who knows who's doing what to whom?" This was the out-of-control feeling that prompted the higher guides of the light under the Prime Directive of the All That Is to come in and help to sort things out, to uplift and energize and do whatever they can to help you, because it has been clear for some time that you had reached the point of no return and that great quantities of help had to be brought in to "save" you. Saving you means having you remember where you came from and who you truly are.

Regarding the entities that have caused everything to go awry, you may have been told that in this time of accelerated light they will be expelled from your experience. You may also have heard that they're kicking up a lot of dust as they're escorted out of your influence. You could call this "poor sportsmanship." They are like teams, players who know they can't hope to win but who are determined to fight as hard and as long as possible, just on principle, even though they now know that they're up against something unconquerable, which is the case.

The Forces of Light are now so great, and there are so many awakened, that it's not possible for Light to lose. The greatest challenge remains how to spark the awakening process in those who are still asleep. We count on you and on those of you who have bridged to us and have allowed us to come through. Although it's hard for you to imagine that you have power that we do not, in truth we count on you to help us with this mission as Light Workers, for you can do it in a way that we can't. Because you are becoming aware of your Exalted Self at the same time you are living in this dimension with people who are still asleep, you have a way to reach them that is not possible for us, since we're not living in bodies in your plane. Therefore, we rely on you most humbly to help us. We honor you and revere your special role in the Ascension of ALL beings . . . of ALL dimensions.

CHAPTER TWELVE:

Soul Retrieval—Return to Harmonic Resonance

Here is Melora's explanation of how soul retrieval is done with the help of our personal guides, angelic beings, and ascended masters. This information gives us insight into how soul retrieval works energetically from higher dimensions.

We are indeed Melora. We are of the light, and we are pleased to work with you. Now—to explain how the guides do "soul retrieval": Recall that, energetically, the vibration of wholeness and love are essentially the same. Any vibration that is separate from the Whole can be said to be inharmonic, or even dis-eased. The affinity that you feel for another person is a matter of resonance, is it not? Where your resonance is the same, or similar enough, that you don't feel a disparate quality, you don't feel a separation. What you term as love often is that feeling of oneness, which is a very small glimpse of the Oneness that is.

When performing soul retrieval we're dealing with separation, and in addressing the problem of separation, or fragmentation, we work energetically with changing the resonance. What you would term "attracting" the fragment back to the Core Soul we would term as bringing their resonances ever closer and closer together until they are the same energetically. You can also call this *communication.* Remember that when you really communicate with someone they are "getting it," and you are in accord, are in one, with what is being communicated, are you not? **Thus, you can term soul retrieval as setting up a bridge of communication.** Again, the method is an energetic sounding that brings the fragment and the Core Soul into resonance. So you can term it communication and you can term it resonance—the fragment(s) and the Core Soul are now harmonic instead of dissonant. They are now the same, instead of a separate, "tone."

In order to get a person's first critical fragment back we enhance, or particularize, the person's resonance with our energy work, as you would term it, so that it closer approximates, for a time, the resonance of the critical fragment that we understand is the one to bring back first. Then that fragment's resonance and the Core Soul's resonance are modulated again to the healthier harmonic. It might be that the Core Soul, not just the fragment, needs adjusting. They are, nonetheless, adjusted and modulated in a sort of courtship, a sort of dance of subtle modulation until there is a harmonic that is the healthiest or "whole-est" harmonic for both. In that harmonic they achieve their reunion.

Now, as we extend from that, the resonance of the Core Soul has become modified, because it is now greater. It has this fragment back and has been adjusted for this reunion. In that resonance it can "call" to the next fragment. Then it calls to the next, and to the next, and so on, as the resonance adapts, modulates and changes between them in this courtship of the parts and the Core Soul. Then this resonance in the Core Soul changes subtly, achieves more of a wholeness as the parts are re-integrated, is now greater than, more whole than, it was before, and therefore can now attract each next "fragment." With the help of your guides, that "courtship" of modulation takes place. Again, this is at an energetic level, and at the level of wholeness, love, and light at which all things operate at maximum efficiency.

We're modulating both, together, until they achieve one arc, as in a voice match. We can do this energetically at levels, and at "speeds," that are not otherwise possible. (*Speed*, here, really means that you're not experiencing a time factor in the integration process as you would if you took the shamanic route.) Not all guides are adept at doing this. We would suggest that it's not something to mess around with—that one needs to know who is really able to do this and work very carefully. There is also an adjustment period, even in doing soul retrieval energetically.

If you were to look at soul retrieval from the guides' point of view, because we do not see images the way you do, it would be much as if you were blindfolded and you were in a sensory deprivation unit, and someone played a tone that you could not hear, but you could feel the vibration of the tone in your body. We will add something else that may help you: As with a dolphin using sonar to locate food, we first sound, as it were (without meaning that we hear something). *Using a sonic method almost, we sound out where the fragment is and locate it by the energy "signature" that ties it to the Core Soul. Its signature is the same as that of the Core Soul.*

This is how we know that we have the right one, or ones. Then, almost with a sonic wave—without sound but with a sonic energy—we [*snaps fingers*] sound, and we find the fragment(s). Once we've located each fragment we're able to determine, by its resonance, which is the optimal one to bring back first and then what the sequence would be. It's almost a gradation, the way there are different hertz/megahertz frequencies for each tonal value. It's just something energetically that we can identify automatically.

The fragments are tied to the Core Soul energetically . . . with that signature . . . almost the way DNA is your signature and yours is unlike anyone else's. They are "attached" by what you could term an "energetic bridge," but remember that the fragment and the Core Soul normally have no consciousness of each other.

That's the problem: the separation in consciousness. Setting up communication makes you conscious of each other—you as the Core Soul and the fragment as a signature part of you that needs to be reunited with your Core Soul.

Thus, energy-to-energy, there is a communication and understanding and clarity about what belongs with what. There's a signature trace that belongs to the Core Soul. We identify it; we track it. Now we start modulating the resonance of each so they come more into alignment. We are able to determine where the "healthy" resonance is and to bring both the Core Soul and the fragment to that ideal reunion. We do the same with each successive soul fragment.

They're not just "floating around somewhere 'out there'." They're right here [just over the heart chakra]—in the intersections of your etheric web. They have no beliefs; they have no dynamic consciousness. They're encapsulated. They're stuck in time; they're static . . . from the point at which they left. It would be almost like a person who after an accident has memory only of the recent past, or you have one memory that plays over and over again, but there's nothing beyond that.

The soul fragment is in that kind of static state, almost as though whatever it took with it at the point of trauma is all that it has consciousness of. There's no consciousness of the connection to the Core Soul. The only reality it experiences is whatever trauma provoked it to leave. That is its main and, usually, only memory. *You can see how traumatic it must be as the fragment returns to the Core Soul if one is integrating it by oneself, or even in therapy what difficulty might be experienced emotionally and psychologically, considering what memories that fragment is bringing back to the consciousness of the person housing the Core Soul.*

It may interest you to know that the Ascended Masters and guides helping Jyoti were given permission to select the soul fragments in a certain order. Working with the higher wisdom created a sort of "domino effect." With these critical parts back, a couple of them (which surprised Jyoti intellectually as being that critical to the process), in a certain order, started magnetically to call to the other fragmented soul aspects that were still "out there." Merely starting the process magnetically calls to those parts because, remember: The Whole keeps trying to form. The fragments magnetically *want* to come back to the Whole.

The lost soul aspect has no consciousness until it is reunited with the Core Soul, which has access to the "data banks," has access to the intellect, the mind. The Core functioning of the consciousness of the being is with the Core Soul. So when the fragment is approached, it's going to be in a state of trauma, remembering only what was happening at the point at which it left. When it is "approached," a communication connection is then made to the core consciousness, and then it remembers everything. (However, *the aspect doesn't have conscious access to the Core Soul until it is fully integrated.*)

During soul retrieval it becomes conscious that it has been separate and that the desire of the Core Soul is to bring it to union, or reunion. This is because of the fragment's experience as an energy essence extension of the Core Soul (separated in consciousness while it's a fragment). The newly returned fragment suddenly "realizes" that it has been separate in consciousness from the Core Soul. It now realizes that its separation is due to the event of which it has such an intense memory. Then, in the consciousness connection with the Core Soul, the lost soul aspect exaggerates what will happen if it returns, because now it realizes that it left its Core Soul as a result of the traumatic event.

Now a fear starts: "Well, if I return, then I'm going to experience this again. If I stay, this is all I'm remembering now, but at least it's not going to happen again. If I return it's going to happen again." The fear element is one of the greatest impediments, and so the shaman, for example, coaxes it by saying "Well, here's how good it's going to be when you come back," and the Core Soul says, "I promise that things are much better now, and I'll protect you," and whatever else one says in full consciousness that this is what the fragment needs.

Again, consciousness is the key. The Core Soul consciousness is saying, "I understand that you're going to be freaked out," and so on. So there's this negotiating (as when you do the process in the shamanic way) on a conscious level, usually with thoughts, words and emotions. *There can be much fear attached in the reëntry of the lost soul aspect, and the memory in the physical body has to be released from the physical body at the cellular level.*

It is different when we're working *energetically* with the resonance—when you're working with the etheric body, that, then, heals the physical body. When you're working only energetically with the guides, we're doing the resonance modulation without running information through the brain, without your experiencing "Oh, my God! I'm so terrified, and I'm having nightmares, and I'm having emotional reactions because of the fragments coming back, and I'm trying to integrate, only I'm going through this depression," and so on.

You see, that is the modulating process, but *it's much slower in the shamanic way because it's being directed through the consciousness of the person.* That's why there's more suffering involved in [the shamanic way] of integration; that's why the process takes much longer, in your terms, and so on. As we assist energetically, we send love and radiant light to replace the darkness, the fear, that the soul aspect felt . . . to neutralize any dark energy that was adhering to the aspect. With every breath out, the residue of that aspect's experience is washed away. We energetically give the person the absolute knowledge and belief that all of her/him is totally of the light. We endeavor to make this as comfortable as possible. We manifest golden light energy for the warmth, the love, and the safety.

After soul retrieval, integration of the returned soul aspects is necessary, and it is our perception that this is what is so difficult when you do it the shamanic way. In the latter, once the retrieval is done, then the client is generally left to go through the rigors of integration on his or her own. We suggest that in having the assistance of guides who specialize in this and who understand this energetically, the process can be much swifter, much more comfortable because of what we termed as the subtle modulations.

As carefully and subtly as we work to modulate both the fragment's resonance and the Core Soul's resonance, there still is an adjustment period. With *any* change that you go through as a human being there is an adjustment period because suddenly what seemed familiar to you is now altered. This is minimized, however, by taking the energetic approach with your high guides of the light rather than by undergoing a process on a linear level in a soul journey—with its psychological and emotional integration of the parts that takes many months to complete—that is often disturbing and that requires much strength on the part of the person undergoing the process. (We're not suggesting that there's only one way to do this. What is appropriate for some is the shamanic route, and so on.)

When you have several "soul fragments" in a particular lifetime and you do not incorporate them, this contributes to "karma" if you are not conscious of those fragments and/or of multi-dimensional lives, which you term "reincarnational." Then for each multi-dimensional life there are soul fragments that need to be brought back. Merging with the Higher Self requires the soul integration process of returning these lost soul aspects. (In case you are wondering, it is not really possible for the integration of soul fragments in a non-incarnated state. If you had some soul fragments missing, you died, and your soul left your body— what you would think of as "past lives" or lost soul aspects—you could not decide NOT to incarnate again. You couldn't just decide NOT to have the fragments retrieved.)

The Core Soul is what would reincarnate because of the laws of what you call karma, which really have to do with where your growth stopped when the body died. If you're unable to achieve that integration in this body in this life, it still must be achieved, so you go to the next incarnation and the work still needs to be done to integrate that. (Also: in each multi-dimensional life—what you term reincarnational lives—there are soul aspects of other beings sharing each of those "past" lives with you; there are also "future" lives and present lives.)

If you still remain unconscious of those other multi-dimensional lives, you bring their "influences" with you to your "next" incarnation, hopefully to awaken you to the reality that they're "out there." We will qualify this: It really more concerns "issues" that are so dramatic and intense in certain lifetimes that they carry over to other lifetimes. **Say you have this issue going on in five or six lifetimes, and you're not "getting it" in any of the lifetimes. It will continue to magnify and goad you intensely, and then, hopefully, at least in one lifetime you will get it. Coming to that consciousness will then filter through the Higher Self (and the Higher Self's growth as a part of the process) to the other lives. Then this issue can be neatly resolved so that you no longer carry it with you.**

If—imagine it . . . you have this "problem" in six lifetimes and you're not getting it . . . you're being very dull, indeed, about the whole thing or very stubborn, or whatever it might be that is keeping you from seeing this. Of course it's going to compound and find expression further, and then it can be sort of nightmarish because the problems resonate back and forth to each life expression until the lessons are learned. This is what this has to do with becoming conscious. *When we say you must become conscious of your multi-dimensional lives we really mean: Become conscious of the unresolved issues you're still carrying.*

There are extreme cases of soul fragmentation in which a person can be "occupied" by another entity, or other entities— unfortunately, usually of what you term "the dark." In schizophrenia, for example, you have the nature of the extreme separation inherent in the term: the *schism*, or split, between the parts and the whole of the Core Soul. Say you have so many pieces and there's some integrity that holds them together. Say you lose 50 "pieces" out of 100. (We're just using this figure for the sake of example; it really doesn't make sense to us). You're still functioning, but people are going to think you're very odd, indeed, at this point. If you lose more than that, however, your personality as expressed is going to become very vague. Actually, you may well be inhabited by negative entities because of the weakness of your will. Because of the breaking down of the integrity of the parts to the whole, then the will may become prey to entities that are "up to no good," as you would term it.

For soul retrieval to occur, a person needs to realize that s/he has fragments and to intend that they return. Without these two requirements, it cannot happen. Now (and know that this a more hopeful answer), for those of you who are conscious of being on an ascension path—and who are consciously working with your guides—with your intent and your consciousness that you do indeed have soul fragments, a sort of pact can be created in which your guides have an understarding. This understanding is that in order for you to ascend, soul retrieval must be done.

Eventually this will be taken care of between you and your guides out of your own consciousness anyway, not even necessarily because you decided one day actually to go through the process of soul retrieval. Although it's rare for parts simply to come back on their own, this can sometimes be achieved with your just being conscious that they might exist and having the intention that your guides help the fragments merge again with you. The consciousness that you may have the lost soul aspects is prerequisite to having this process be possible without assistance. Primarily we wish you to know that we do this energetically.

The illusion of un-wholeness is what we're addressing here, so you simply let go of the illusion of un-wholeness and you automatically have health, love, and everything else you ever dreamed of. However, you are so fond of your illusions. You know: Your ego says, "Well, I have to work really hard for this or I won't deserve it." If you want to make it hard, and your belief system says, "If it's not hard, I'm not going to value it," or whatever other illusions are there, it will indeed be difficult. If you want to buy into its taking longer, you can make it be even harder . . . or you can have it now.

The reason you can have it now is that the Whole exists whether you see it or believe in it. The Whole exists for all time and always—now, and in the past, and in what you call the future. Everything is all there NOW. So all you do is choose to experience the whole thing now, period, instead of just experiencing part of it, but first you have to believe it's possible to do that. **What reality** is, what Totality is, is looking at a hologram and seeing the whole, all the possibilities at one time.

Separation from that union creates the illusion that you can experience this part only between now and five minutes from now, or for this lifetime, or whatever other restrictions you want to put on it, or "until I get well," or "until I have enough money," or "until my mother starts acting like a normal human being." Thus, you can restrict yourself in as many ways as you can imagine, but the simple truth is that you are already whole. You are already well and healthy. Only the illusion of not being whole keeps you from experiencing it.

Relinquishing the illusions *reveals* the wholeness. It's that basic. Do whatever you need to do to set up a session in the light. Bring in all your guides and say, "This is what I want. I am intending that I relinquish anything that's standing in my way of joy, love, and wholeness," and so on. Of course *it CAN happen instantly, but typically there are too many sorts of hidden beliefs back there insisting that this can't happen.*

All of these suggestions are to bring you back to your own sense of control and power over your destiny, and your health, and your wellness, and your wholeness. You start with techniques that you believe are tools you need in order to accomplish something. You can always take the shortcut, however, and then just BE it—or you can use the tools.

CHAPTER THIRTEEN:

Discipline, Compassion & Human Emotion

(excerpts from a workshop in Sedona, Arizona)

We have been hearing recently from so many that they still feel separate from Source Creator, as much "work" as they have done in seeking spiritual attainment. This is a *felt*, not an actual, separation. On some level you know that you have created this separation. In pulling back and separating yourselves and in isolating yourselves in your own psyches, your own spirits, you create the separation instead of maintaining the sphere of union that you enjoy in attending workshops of the type that we support.

We say this not to make you feel bad about yourselves but to offer instruction. This is a learning process for your awareness and consciousness of how powerful you really are in creating your reality. You can choose to create that union, or you can choose in the moment to separate yourself from that union. The question that comes next is: *Why would one choose to separate oneself from this beautiful, loving Source?*

Discipline

The answer is: "the work that is still left to be done." Even choosing to begin a spiritual path takes tremendous courage and discipline. The true meaning of "discipline" is not rapping someone's knuckles with a ruler in parochial school. Discipline means "to learn." This has a Latin root, as in "disciple." There is no value judgment, no connotation of hardship or austerity. It simply means *to learn*.

So . . . courage and discipline on the spiritual path. To learn means "This happens. I make a mistake." One makes many mistakes during each lifetime. To learn means: "I become conscious of what didn't work," what was not beneficial, what was harmful to self or others, what was done for the wrong reasons (however sincere). In that consciousness, one simply then makes the more beneficial, optimal choice the next time. That's all it is.

To learn doesn't mean to flagellate the self: "I thought I got over this five years ago, and now I'm going through it again!" The illusion is that you still haven't learned the lesson. The reality is that there are arms, like octopus arms, and the core issue is like the main body of the octopus. You may have "taken care" of two arms, but there are six left. Do you see? **You keep thinking that you have resolved a certain issue and now here it is, back again. However, what you've done is to go out to the periphery and resolved a *tangential expression* of that issue. You have, perhaps, resolved only some *behavioral* aspect. Yes, you've stopped doing whatever that is, but the core issue still remains.**

In our soul retrieval work we go for the core, so that you no longer have these other "arms" to work with. When you encounter another aspect out here, the appropriate response is now to work with that and to resolve it—not to say: "I must be stupid" or to berate yourself for supposedly revisiting something. It's never the same river, as that saying goes. You may dip your foot into the River Ganges in the same place seconds later, but it's no longer the same river, do you see?

If you start thinking about these situations as opportunities, then you will have more excitement about being given the chance to work with them and to resolve them. As we have said, *growth is ongoing*. Our Jyoti said to us one time: "When you're in a human body, knowing that it goes on and on and on can be pretty depressing." It's as the myth of Sisyphus: Sisyphus is in Hades, rolling that rock up the hill one more time, only to have it roll right back down again. This was the Greeks' notion of Hell. This is also the idea inherent in concepts of reincarnation: "Back again. Didn't do it right. Can't get over this."

Two elements are important here: (1) acknowledging and taking responsibility for the fact that it is you choosing to create these events, including the most uncomfortable ones you can think of and (2) realizing that you have an opportunity to learn and now to choose what's beneficial. These are critical factors in whether you do indeed move on, take your body to Light, and now have your focus in 5th Dimension all the time, instead of just getting glimpses of it.

Compassion

People confuse compassion with empathy, sympathy, and so forth. Compassion is actually much more neutral, and we will tell you why. We will take the word "pity," and we will show you how pity is more about *you* than it is about the one being pitied. In order to pity someone, you first put yourself in their place. You're really saying: "Boy, if I were in [so-and-so's] place, I would feel" . . . such-and-such. You really don't come into compassion in doing that because it's really about you.

When you are in compassion you merely acknowledge that person with love and non-judgment. Now, with pity (and even sometimes with sympathy) there's an odd mixture of emotions, is there not? There's a sort of a repulsion in which you're perhaps thinking: *I really feel sorry for you but please keep away*. Like the transient or the bag lady. You may feel sorry for them and give them money, but you physically recoil. There is judgment in that.

With compassion there is no recoiling. There is no revulsion. You simply reach out with love to the person, exactly as that person is. You do not need to try to make yourself feel more comfortable around that person. That's merely behavior modification.

It is exactly the same in relating to yourself. These are some of the reactions you experience so intensely in desiring, and at the same time recoiling from, the Path of Light, because some uncomfortable things go on as parts of yourself jump out of the woodwork, and as the skeletons come out of the closet and dance and play piano on your head. [laughter] That's the revulsion, because you say, "I want to feel this wonderful, spiritual love and be embraced by it, and yet I'm not willing to acknowledge that I've got to clean my closet, my attic and my basement."

In talking to someone yesterday, our Jyoti said, "What if you took everything out of your attic and your garage, and your basement and closets, and put these things all around the inside of your house in your living area? How would you feel?" [laughter] How would you feel, living among this junk? That's what a number of you are experiencing right now. All of your "junk" is out. You're trying to be in your space, and it's just closing in on you. Our Jyoti said: "Well, what do you do? You have a garage sale. You get the junk out of your house, out on the lawn, and other people might want to use it. Or you take some of it to the Salvation Army, or you throw it in the trash."

This is exactly what would be appropriate to do with some of these things that are "in your face" right now. However, do not confuse these things that are dredged up from your attic, basement and closet with WHO YOU ARE. This is what happens. It is important now that when what our Jyoti calls those "rodent voices" (those tape recordings from your childhood that make you feel bad about yourselves) start gnawing on you, you begin to take charge. You begin to say: "No! That's not true!"

The truth is that you are exalted, beautiful beings of Light and Love, temporarily choosing to be trapped in a body in this thick, gelatinous density you call Earth. **If you "get it"—if, against all odds, you remember that you are divine, if you're able to prevail and transcend and see through the** *illusion* **that you are not divine—you make more spiritual progress than you ever could by remaining in some disembodied state, strumming your harp, and having no challenges whatsoever.**

It is not desirable that you coast somewhere else forever, never changing and never growing. It *is* desirable that you learn, that you remain a disciple, and you do that by starting right now. You start making choices now. We suggest that you don't revisit your mistakes or punish yourself for what has gone on before in your process. Honor your own process. Love the fact that you have the ability to become conscious of yourself as a spiritual being who happens, right now, to be a consciousness focused in a body.

People are often very competitive in the various spiritual communities. This is just succumbing to peer pressure. [laughter] The need for approval, do you see, is a great barrier to true spiritual growth. If Jeshua (the *Christed* One), Buddha, and other great masters had been worried about what people thought of their messages, those messages would never have been delivered! They had good news, and they had bad news, do you see? **People like to hear that they might be able to release karma. People don't want to hear that change and growth are required.**

Some people are even competitive with themselves. They say, "I ought to be farther along," but these things go in cycles. It is not the same river. Even if you say, "I should have known better. I thought I resolved this five years ago" . . . whip, whip, whip (Cat-o'-Nine-Tails). That certainly does not help you grow spiritually. In fact, it sets you back because this is self-abuse.

Human Emotion

It is important not to feel that if you are disturbed or angry, or whatever, it automatically means that you have some demonic possession or something. This is the other aspect of what we wish to talk to you about today, and that is: If you weren't meant to have emotions, you wouldn't be here. If you hadn't chosen to experience the gamut of emotions, you wouldn't be here. Thus, righteous anger, justified anger, is appropriate. However, anger that harms another is inappropriate. Righteous anger would cause you to come to the aid of someone who needs your protection . . . take action on some universal principle—someone being violated. Protecting what you call Civil Rights—the right of a being not to be harmed—can come from righteous anger. An example would be Jeshua's turning over the tables of the money lenders in the temple. So many people believe that Jeshua didn't have human emotions, and it's simply untrue.

We would suggest that the most fruitful way to deal with these emotions is to acknowledge them. In doing so, you de-fuse them. When you deny them you give them power. As an example (as the great J. Krishnamurti[24] pointed out), all human beings have the potential for violence, and so anyone who says "I am not violent" is fibbing. If you want non-violence, you don't deny or hate violence; you acknowledge it. You say: "You know? I have a violent streak within me." When you say this, the violence actually goes away. When you deny it, the pressure builds.

What we're saying is that when you're on a spiritual path and an emotion that you judge to be "non-spiritual" occurs, and you deny that that emotion has a right to exist in you if you're truly spiritual, you shut yourself off from consciousness of your own divinity. Your own judgment of what you consider to be inappropriate behavior for a "spiritual" being separates you right in that moment. We know what you're thinking: "It's easy for you to say, Melora." [laughter]

Our Jyoti has said that to us a number of times over the past years. However, these are not absolutes, and we agree with you. You go in stages. Growth means that you develop from some "point" to some other "point." When you were first learning to walk, what would have happened if, when you fell down after trying to take the first step, your parents said: "You are SO BAD!" Actually, they said: "Good boy!" or "Come on, Susie! That's it."

---

[24] *The Flight of the Eagle*, by J. Krishnamurti. Harper, 1971. 180 pages.

Such love. This is the way WE feel in looking toward you. We're saying, gently: "Come on. Come on. You can do it." You can do it, and we are not the ones "punishing" you. You are punishing yourselves for "falling down."

Think of where you are on your path right now, and where you will continue to go, because you never really "get there." There's not some specific point that you're going to reach. Only in your own mind is there such a situation. So look at yourselves with compassion. This is not self-pity. This is: "You know what? I've really come a long way. I want to acknowledge myself for what I have accomplished. I could be a schizophrenic now because of all I've gone through, but I'm not. I took my courage and pulled myself up by my bootstraps, and I'm strong. I'm courageous, and, yes, I still make mistakes. But, by golly, I've done some pretty miraculous things, considering what I've had to work with."

So when you examine yourselves, start being fair. Start bringing up these other things that you've done, against very great odds, that are so fabulous. Look at those things, "for goodness' sake." When you think of us, these beings that you perceive as so high above you, you sever your connections with us by thinking, "I am less than . . ." You've been so conditioned to think this is ego. This is reality. When you think of us, whatever you think of us as being, know that the reality is that we're saying: "Come on, you can make it. Come on. One more step."

We thank you for listening. Wishing you great Joy of the Light, we are Melora.

APPENDIX A

Melora & The Author's Soul Group

(excerpts from a private session)

LR: Jyoti and I would like some clarification . . . as stated in another session . . . when she referred to you as her "Golden Angel," you said that was true at the time, and that she was the *seed* of that which we recognize that not everyone would be but that that is her angelic lineage.

MELORA: It was *her* interpretation at the time that we were the Golden Angel and that she was the seed of us as the Golden Angel. When she said, "Are you my Golden Angel?" we were emphasizing the word "golden" and "angel" in our Oneness as being true, but we were hesitating about giving her that sensation that she recognizes as meaning "Yes," understanding that, for a time, she might not be conscious of exactly what that core relationship represents. Thus, in *her* understanding of us as her Higher Self, she placed herself in the position of seed self to us as Golden Angel.

As we went on further to say, *she* is the Higher Self of which we are what you would term a peripheral "part" in consciousness, so that where we are in consciousness, for example, allows us to give the impression of channeling through her, whereas what is really going on (as you so perceptively understood) is that she is *remembering* . . . we are helping her in our role on the periphery, if you will, to remember that *she* is the Higher Self. You understand that in the overall perspective we are One, but for the time being, at the time, when she asked if we were her Golden Angel, "Are you my Future Self?" and so on, what we were trying to say is that when she is "where we are now," she may well be greater than we are. Understand that all this is simultaneous; we are all operating on all levels at one time. This is how she can be the Higher Self expressed as her, here.

LR: Regarding what you just said, Jyoti's being the Higher Self, also connected with the Golden Angel, with you on the periphery—

MELORA: She *is* the Golden Angel . . .

LR: And she is the Golden Angel; all is One. Then where does Jyoti's *personality*—the smaller self, so to speak—fit into this? Is all this drawing together in the center of a sphere, so to speak?

MELORA: Let us express it this way: As we understand that we are aware, there are great beings who have chosen to come into embodiment, particularly at this time, to do the work that is here, and it is work that is not possible to do in a disembodied state. Where she has come from is a very high angelic realm. This is her Core Soul, and so this is an example of a being from that angelic hierarchy actually choosing to come into form in a body on the earth. This is not the same as having a Higher Self create seed selves. Therefore, she is *not* a Seed Self of a Higher Self; she is a Higher Self *embodied*.

LR: . . . within a shell, and because she's within a form, she also has to deal with the lower personality, as we all do?

MELORA: Yes. Because of the density of 3-D reality.

LR: So what is really going on now is that which we might call the lower bodies? The personality, the lower mental and emotional bodies are now being merged.

MELORA: Yes.

LR: They are giving themselves, willingly, over to the Higher Self for the greater work, so that instead of the ego and personality being in opposition, she is willingly allowing that to dissolve and to merge.

MELORA: Yes, and the way we would put it is that she is remembering more and more where she came from, remembering her stature as a being. She has made a "sacrifice" in coming to this body and in having chosen a life that was very rigorous and very traumatic so that she could constantly be triggered in sensitivity—so that she wouldn't get too enmeshed in family, and children, which would have distracted her. Remaining alone has made her more focused on her three-dimensional life, and so she essentially has chosen a life in which she s always had to be on her toes.

Understand that in making this sacrifice (as have all who have embodied now from higher states of being) it is necessary to do this so that all are linked, "vertically," through to the center of the Earth as you have heard it described, so that ALL dimensions can merge in consciousness. Without coming into the body, there are just those guides so-called "out here" who impulse you to do this, that, or the other. However, there is no direct energetic connection with us—there is an embodied anchor for that consciousness. You see? In 3-dimensional reality—to anchor that.

As you perceive it, it might be more appropriate to term expansion of consciousness as "remembrance," an acceleration of remembrance of the totality of that state of being that "was" enjoyed before coming into the body, before coming into this very dense reality. So it is *recapturing*, remembering the joy, the lightness and the love, and the heart, and so on.

Although our Jyoti isn't very confident about the "progress" she has made, we can assure her that she has performed miracle after miracle of consciousness considering what traps people in 3-D. Many entities do not wish, ever, to take the risk to come into body because they get trapped, as you read in the book by Solara[25]... fear of being trapped and that entity's never being able to return to the light. So these are very courageous acts of those who have done this.

Melora (of The Council of Four)

LR: You also refer to yourself as a guide, so we need some clarification.

MELORA: Yes, and there has been much confusion here, and Jyoti has asked this question of other channels, and so on and so on. Understand that in each step of the process of her consciousness what we have said is appropriate for that step. It is actually *she* who chose to have an understanding that we are her Higher Self because of a relationship of her understanding of having information coming from a "higher consciousness" than hers. Although we could say that as a being she is higher than we, at the time when she began to channel (and at various times in the process), our relationship to her has been as a guide of higher consciousness—

---

[25] EL*AN*RA: *The Healing of Orion*, by Solara. Star-Borne Unlimited, 1991. 271 pages.

meaning, a consciousness that has more remembrance of who it is than she had at that time.

So we say that "Consciousness is all." Her consciousness at certain points would not allow her to remember, believe, and accept that *she*, in fact, is the higher being. Thus, what she has described as our being her Higher Self is really her consciousness at certain times about our relationship to her—a description of her *interpretation* of our relationship to her—a consciousness that appears to be higher than hers because it has access to information that she, in the density of 3-D, has not had.

The real question here seems to be: "Okay. Did you, Melora, say you were her Higher Self, and why did you say that if it isn't true?" As you know, we always try to answer questions as clearly as possible and, as we said, at the time we first "channeled" to her on her birthday and she said, "Are you my Golden Angel?" . . . as we put it, "golden" and "angel" applied to our resonance as well, and we offered the name *Melora* to put her in touch with the wing of her soul group that is so important.

In the need for the human brain to have these clear-cut boundaries and these black-and-white names that simply don't exist for us, and in the name of what is true for each fluid moment, everything that we have said is true in that moment. However, it always changes—as soon as the consciousness expands, the very qualities of the truth take on greater proportion, greater dimension, greater color. The truth is that ALL of this is true because of the Oneness. Thus, it is difficult to say we are her Higher Self; we are not her Higher Self. **Incidentally, *we* have not been embodied as Melora, *directly*.**

LR: Well, *this* makes better sense to me, thank you, than any-thing else so far, because I, as you know, have had questions and somehow, wherever I'm coming from, have had diffi-culty with some of this because knowingness seems to be much more in accord with what you have just said, and I thank you for explaining this. I'm sure we're going to have more questions as we move along.

The Council of Four

MELORA: Jyoti is getting an education here, as well, in this process, you see, and this started yesterday in your discus-sion. Again, all of this is also true—in the Oneness. It's just shifting perspectives, and by looking at this object from this side, or underneath, from above, from that side . . . and so, in the interpretation of Higher Self vs. guide or whatever, you're simply looking at the Oneness from "the other side."

LR: Well, I have a much easier time with looking at it from just one side. Can you briefly describe the others of The Council of Four? And then briefly state their purpose and how they're working here, as Jyoti is searching for a tape from a more than a year ago of a session in which you do just that. In fact, it may have changed somewhat since then.

Ocala, [26] *of The Council of Four*

MELORA: Yes. You see, if Jyoti had found the tape we would not be having this session today. [laughs] All right. So as Jyoti *did* understand yesterday, there is a sort of balancing of "talents." We consider Ocala, whom she channeled as a prelude to linking with us[27], to be our sister resonance. She is of the angelic resonance. She has chosen to express in her work in what you term "The Great White Brotherhood" (which is so much vaster than anybody has ever even explained, because it includes the entire angelic realm and not just the higher angelic realm, and this is expressed in many different ways: strength, compassion, merging as we express it, and so on). Ocala is specifically "talented" in making sure that what you experience as negative forces and energies stay in their place and that they don't interfere.

Ocala is a sentinel, a guardian of the energetic space as we do our work not only with our Jyoti's consciousness but also with all her various parallel, multi-dimensional expressions. Ocala is the protector who, as they say in Biblical terms, "casts out demons." So she keeps that vibration of sage and holy water and that resonance of beautiful light so that nothing of a lower vibration can come and interfere. That is very much her role. As subtle and angelic as she is, and as sweet

---

[26] Ocala was first introduced to me as my guide from The Great White Brotherhood in February of 1993, although no name was given. In a session with another channel in Longmont, CO, on 3/1/94 I received her name. Here are descriptions of Ocala: "You know the one called Ocala? She's got a robe that's silver and [the robe] has four lines [running vertically]." (Actually, before this session I had awakened from a nap and had seen Ocala in this robe—complete with the four vertical lines!) "She says she's [a] 'sister'."

[27]During a session in January of 1995, Melora said: "We have been working with our Jyoti for quite some time, coming to her in the form of her own thoughts."

as her energy is perceived, she is not somebody "to mess with." She does not need to be fierce because her very vibration thwarts and neutralizes anything of an inferior vibration. She doesn't need to use spears, or swords, or shields of the light—her very energy makes it impossible for anything of a lesser vibration to exist within her sphere.

All right. We have said that Jyoti is of an angelic vibration. It could be said that ALL the members of The Council of Four are of that vibration. There are many different expressions of angelic energy. Just as you gravitate around those who appreciate and emanate beauty and refinement, there are those of the angelic realm who are drawn to those of a similar resonance. This is what you experience in your soul group.

Both we and Ocala have been perceived as having bronze, or even copper-colored, "skin." Again, this is the orange ray, the second ray, but having the quality of energy that makes it iridescent, with the effect of the energy swirling, and so on. The "coyness" that some have experienced in Ocala is typical of those who resonate more strongly to the angelic frequencies because there is a joyful mischief and an unwillingness to be pinned down to one image or one kind of energy experience. So this is Ocala.

Bilá, of The Council of Four

MELORA: Bilá, whom some people have seen as blue[28], some as male or female, or androgynous. Bilá was also embodied as an anchor-point lifetime such as this in very ancient Tibet, and she is interpreted as Tibetan because of that. S/he, expresses through the sacred dance and mudras, and it is pos-

---

[28] Blue (as in the energy of Krishna, as he is depicted) is that very third-eye kind of energy as expressed through the skin energetically—a deep blue-white color.

sible with the dance to do healing—not only for yourself but for others—in just your arm movements, as you [meaning, LR] know with your own work with the spirals.

Just doing parallel arm movements *over* someone can cut through a lot of dreck in the auric field, because you're working with the energetic versions of the body. What you term "etheric" and "auric" are energetic—even the mental body. As you may know, if you pass your hand over the crown, you can cut the person's physical energy in half. You can do muscle testing to demonstrate that this is true. When you're doing sacred dance and mudras as Bilá does (in fact, she came into the healing session with St. Germain, [another channel and her guide], and ourselves in the fall of 1994 when we were doing the soul retrieval work and physical healing on them), as we were "channeling" through Jyoti, Bilá was channeling the arm movements and the mudras. The mudras have great power, not only in the body of the one doing them but also when being performed through the channel, then the mudras have the ability to impart that particular kind of energy to the other person.

Our Jyoti is still only in semi-belief one way or the other about it. However, she understands that in "channeling" Bilá, Ocala and Athena,[29] and in linking with ourselves, she makes it possible for us to merge in a way that otherwise would not be possible.

LR: Excellent. Thank you.

---

[29] Athena is discussed in Chapter Eight.

APPENDIX B

The Author's Initial Soul Retrieval

Because I had read Sandra Ingerman's book[30], I was aware that soul retrieval is possible. Since at that time I had only begun to channel, I did not know how to do soul retrieval for myself, and so I sought the help of Mary H. For more than 25 years, Mary has been working with a number of processes that clear and heal the four lower bodies. Although she maintained that she had never used her healing techniques for soul retrieval, she said she would be willing to give it a try.

I approached Mary H. in October 1994 over the phone to initiate my own soul retrieval process. I'm very conscious that I was guided to ask her, and I'm very conscious that her role, on the human level, is that oftentimes we, as humans, can help each other in ways our guides can't help us on the energetic level. For example: Just the physical touch in various kinds of body work and the firsthand understanding of the human dilemma can be critical in being receptive to treatment.

As I told Mary at that time, I had been given the name of a sha-man in some other state, but I just couldn't get in to the idea of going through soul retrieval with a shaman. As I recall, the role Mary would play was to discern, with the help of Ascended Mas-

---

[30] *Soul Retrieval: Mending the Fragmented Self*, by Sandra Ingerman. Harper, 1991. 221 pages.

ters and angels, the critical "soul fragments" and also the optimal order in which to bring them back.

I asked Mary to describe how she was given information about each successive soul fragment. As I remember, she "got" that we could bring back various parts, and she asked if this particular one was appropriate to bring back. She gave me some insight or clue, and instantly I seemed to know which part that was and what age it was. I talked about the fragment that, because of the trauma of childhood sexual abuse, took with it my ability to visualize. Mary dowsed her menus and was guided to use St. Germain's "Prayer of the Violet Flame."[31]

Once Mary got permission to work on my three-year-old fragment, she asked the beings with whom she was working what the priority would be to retrieve it. Then she suggested that I explore flower essences[32] (to take on the physical level) to find what would be most appropriate for integrating this fragment. For my three-year-old fragment Mary also did a "MAP"[33] Session and what she calls "Expansions #1 and #2." (This is integration from "Circles of Life[34]" that was sent to her to expand my auric field.)

At this point we were still working with my fragment from when I was three years old (in the current lifetime). This is amaz-

---

[31] "I am the Violet Flame—in action in me now. I am the Violet Flame—to Light, alone, I bow. I am the Violet Flame, blazing like the Sun. I am God's sacred power, freeing everyone."

[32] Flower essences are distillations of actual plants and flowers. Like those of crystals, their energy frequencies are subtle but powerful. It is yet another example of how the Earth provides natural and resonant, rather than synthetic, remedies, to address virtually any health problem.

[33] *MAP: The Co-Creative White Brotherhood Medical Assistance Program*, 2nd Ed., by Machaelle Small Wright. Perelandra, Ltd., 1994. 317 pages.

[34] After 25 years of study and experimentation, Dorothy Espiau created the Circles of Life program in 1987 to accelerate personal transformation. This re-education program aids in harmonizing discordant energies of the brain, mind and body.

ing to me (and it was amazing at the time): that Mary asked the Ascended Masters and angels to give me the *vibrational* quality—all energetic—of certain flower essences. Then she said it represents "I Am God," about "wisdom/power/love"; it is said to promote total integration: "chalice of light." This is what Mary speaks of as being reunited with your consciousness of your wholeness and Oneness with God. Then she asked the Ascended Masters to send me the vibration of chicory: "Reunion with God." Again, this theme: ascension/consolidation. We climb a few stairs, then we rest. Then we climb a few more stairs.

At this point, Mary talked about "the language of the heart." She apparently was directed to have me scribble out my emotions as they were coming out. First I was really mental and verbal; I avoided the real nitty-gritty. I wrote: "choking," "rage," "pain," "confusion," and so forth. Then Mary said, "You need to do some drawings or something" because I wasn't letting myself really get down to it. I started drawing zig-zaggy lightning things, spirals and a tornado. When Mary said I was finally getting down to it, what I was drawing was painfully intense. [*See the graphic, right.*]

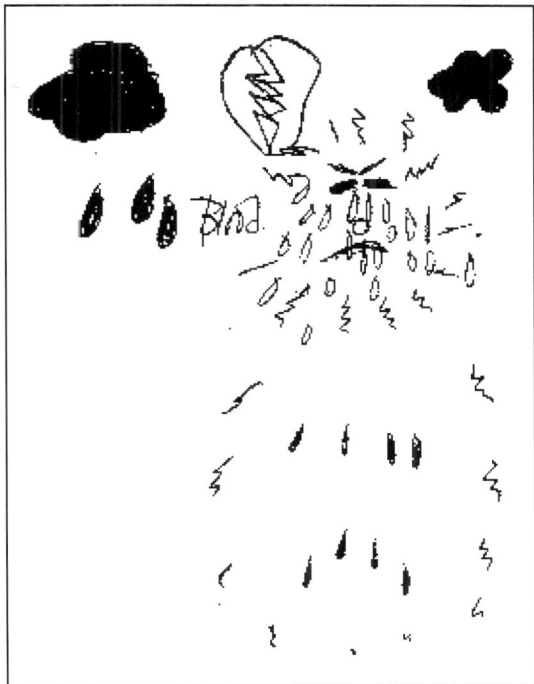

I was drawing drops of blood, sharp-angled things—all those tears of my three-year-old fragment. I looked at her face, those black clouds, and her broken heart at the top of the drawing. I thought: *My God! Is this the way she feels?* At this point Mary said I was truly working at the "language of the heart."

But look at where I started. From writing the words "It hurts!" "This is ugly." "I don't understand." "It's disgusting." And then these sort of vague, abstract things. Then really, really getting down to this. This is three-year-old raw-ness here. At that point Mary instantly said, "Now we're really getting where we need to be in this." It's uncanny that Mary was able to determine, across the phone line, exactly when I got to this point.

(excerpts from an early 1995 interview with Mary H.)

MH: Well, I was asking those who were guiding me to tell me when I had done enough release.

JYOTI: Do you hear the guides speak to you.? Or do you just know?

MH: It's through the dowsing[35]. I kept checking, and when I got a "yes," I knew I had released enough on paper.

JYOTI: That was a fast process to get to that point. And then you encouraged me to look into homeopathic remedies[36] if I was guided to do so. Then we worked further with my three-year-old. This was very intense because we were going on in a multi-layered fashion regarding what to do for her. We moved to the vibrational version of two Bach flower essences: centaury and rock water. Centaury: "for being over-anxious to please, being dominated by others—victim, being taken advantage of." And

---

[35] After much training to be able to remain neutral, and to avoid interference from forces outside themselves, dowsers are able accurately to use a pendulum to verify "yes" and "no" answers to non-layered questions.
[36] Homeopathy is like taking the "hair of the dog that bit you." Based on the principle that "like cures like," homeopathic remedies are taken in extremely minute amounts: normally one part of the remedy to around 1,000,000,000,000 parts of water. Results can be rapid, complete and permanent if the correct homeopathic remedy is used.

rock water: "being too strict with self in daily life, struggling toward an ideal as an example to others." Then you determined that after the MAP Session was complete, we didn't need to do any more for my three-year-old part. For the next fragment your dowsing determined that you should do the Johrei[37] work.

In the next part of your soul retrieval work with me you got that the issues involved neglect, abandonment and deprivation. From this I knew that the next fragment was my five-year-old. There was something about my pneumonia and almost drowning.

MH: I dowsed my list of issues to find which ones were involved.

JYOTI: Then you sent me the three gifts . . . the three balls of light. How did you know to do that?

MH: That's on my "menu" sheet, and I was led, through the dowsing, to send the three balls of light to you for the specific purpose of healing this particular fragment.

JYOTI: The next fragment had to do with something traumatic I went through when I was 31. [I had undergone two big traumas relating to my reproductive system during that year.] You clued me into it by telling me that you were guided to have the energy of the Rune symbol of Fertility sent to me. I knew immediately that this also was related to my childhood sexual abuse, a past life in which I died in childbirth, and the fact that, in my current life, my own mother and I both almost died when I was born Cesarean. All of this is a circle, including my mother's own experience of fear and anger over giving birth to me. As I understand it, these sorts of issues are energetically imprinted on us. My mother's lifelong anger about how painful my birth was, and the rest of

---

[37] *Johrei*, a Japanese therapy, was developed in the early 20th century by Mokichi Okada, founder of the Church of World Messianity. This spiritual healing system is used to rid the body of toxins by directing Divine energy to the client. Toxins are then released through the kidneys.

this, was imprinted back-and-forth, in various ways. You were guided to have me ask the light of God to transform the incidents.

MH: I am still amazed at how they get these messages through—that I don't have to know, but that if it's to be known, I can make the connection.

JYOTI: And "self-forgiveness," "no self-judgment," was what you told me was appropriate for this issue.

MH: At that point we just got quiet and totally submitted to light.

JYOTI: There was one more fragment involving the issue of betrayal, which I recognized as a past-life issue.

MH: And I set up a distant session after we got off the phone, using pyramid paper. When I do this, I also read down the menu sheet to find out what to put on the pyramid paper.

JYOTI: As I understand it, the pyramid structure is pyramids-within-pyramids-within-pyramids. They amplify energetically whatever you put on there, whether it's an affirmation or healing.

MH: Yes, and I was directed to set this up for a specified number of days.

After this initial soul retrieval session, my mother went into a downward spiral. She stopped eating. After about two weeks, a neighbor who hadn't seen her for awhile asked the landlord to go in and see if my mother was all right. She was lying on the floor, her body temperature at around 89 degrees. She was immediately hospitalized.

excerpts from a 12/30/94 session)

EN: I understand. Okay. Let's shift a little bit. I would like to ask about Jyoti and her mother and the recent soul fragments that have returned, two of which her mother had and was living on the essence of.

MELORA: We are receiving *three*. This has not been pointed out. These have come back more recently, and we are getting three.

EN: Have all the fragments returned?

MELORA: Yes.

EN: How is the return of the fragments from her mother affecting her mother, and can you elaborate on this?

MELORA: Yes. We would like to go first to the origin of the soul fragmenting. Jyoti remembered in a hypnotic regression state floating over her mother's body and looking her in the face. (We will help you understand why we are referring to this now. Also: It is important for Jyoti to remember that she re-experienced this consciously.) Remember that an infant does not understand that it is separate from its mother until a certain point in growth, as you would term it. She saw herself floating above her mother and peering into her mother's face, and thought that she was looking into her own face at first—did not feel that she was separate.

What Jyoti was experiencing was that both of them almost died at the time of her birth. She was born surgically, by Cesarean, and her mother almost chose to leave the earth at that time. It was too hard on her physical body. Jyoti and her mother were both in danger at the same moment, and there was a time in which both of them might not have made it. At that moment, for some reason, Jyoti's soul wanted to live, her strength exceeded her mother's, even that early, at the time of birth, and Jyoti chose to give her mother part of her essence so that her mother could stay alive. That was the first fragment. This was how long ago, at birth, she started giving her mother pieces of herself.

Then as what you call a "toddler," Jyoti also gave her mother another soul part to try to sustain her in some way. The third part we are not getting clearly.

167

EN: Without those missing parts, will her mother survive?

MELORA: Not if she, on the soul level, does not choose to be healed in some way. Not unless she has a consciousness of a soul-level intent to survive in this life. That could change. It doesn't look good right *now*. Jyoti is in no way responsible. She has every right to have her soul aspects returned.

EN: Is there something that Jyoti can do . . .

MELORA: [gently] No. Nothing.

EN: Is there something that *anyone* can do, or is it up to the individual concerned at this point?

MELORA: It is totally up to her mother, and we sense that a deeper part of your question is: What's going on with the soul parts now? We would like to answer that. We think you are experiencing some of that process now. It's not something we recommend Jyoti go through alone, and we are very appreciative that you are helping her because this is, indeed, what's happening.

Just after this session I phoned Mary H. and asked her to call in the Ascended Masters to help my mother. After hearing the consensus that, on the soul level, my mother did not want soul retrieval done because she was afraid it would be too painful, I thought I might know of a way to help her. I asked Mary to petition the Ascended Masters and angels to help bring back to my mother only those soul fragments that could give her vitality and joy. In turn, for my mother I did distant Reiki. Apparently, on the soul level my mother made the choice to accept the tremendous help that was sent to her. In Santa Barbara, my sister and uncle were amazed at the overnight change in my mother. My sister, decidedly not a believer in esoteric healing arts, said: "I don't know what you all are doing out there, but it looks a lot like a miracle to us."

APPENDIX C

Past-Life Information & Merging for the Author

A Life in 18th-Century France

(excerpts from a mid-October 1994 session with another channel's guide)

GUIDE: This is about a lost soul aspect that was retrieved first. It was separated in a prior life. It was not broken off in *this* life.

JYOTI: And why was that brought back first?

GUIDE: Your guides were focusing on your ascension process. This was the first one to initiate the retrieval of the rest.

JYOTI: What other life was that? Can you tell me the sort of identity in that life?

GUIDE: It was a past lifetime in France.

JYOTI: In the 1700s?

GUIDE: Um hmm. In your grief about your mother and about deciding not to marry the man you loved, something happened. It was more than sadness that made a part of you flee.

JYOTI: As I experienced this in a hypnotic regression[38] I felt a duty to stay with this man who had been so good to me after I was orphaned, and therefore renounced what I felt would be great happiness with this young man I loved very much. What caused the part to take off? Was it the business with where I couldn't read my mother's diary and tears were streaming down my face?

GUIDE: There is something threatening about that in some way.

JYOTI: Is this something that I need to discover for myself? I don't know if I need to have the *knowledge* of what made that part of that life leave or if, in having come back, that process is complete.

GUIDE: Most of the process with that is complete, and it is mostly integrated. There has been much healing with what caused that to happen. It's already healed in other dimensions.

JYOTI: Does this also regard my issues with my mother in *this* lifetime? Feeling abandoned and orphaned, not having had the nurturing of a mother and feeling very alone without a family?

GUIDE: —but feeling threatened in some way. Survival? Threatened in that "past" life, as you say. The French life is a more appropriate way to describe this.

JYOTI: I have no recollection of that.

GUIDE: It's not necessary to really investigate. The knowledge that this is already healed on most levels, and has already been integrated, is all you really need to know. To pursue the knowledge of what really happened might be counterproductive. It might create more of that same sadness experienced in that time zone, and having this aspect already integrated within your being now, and

---

[38] In 1979 with Sharry Edwards in Athens, OH, I relived having been the ward of a kindly and wealthy, elderly gentleman in this lifetime.

recalling that and dwelling in that time zone (the reason why it left) may tend to push it out again.

JYOTI: Okay. So that aspect is comfortable in having been integrated, and so there's scme comfort for her in this process?

GUIDE: Um hmm. What *is* necessary to know is that it did involve forgiveness.

JYOTI: Okay. Thank you.[39]

A Life in Ancient China

(excerpts from a private session)

Jyoti would like more information about her traumatic life in China.

MELORA: Yes. There has been much resistance to remembering this because this is the severest case of sexual abuse and torture of any of her lifetimes, [gently] including *this* one. It resonates throughout her incarnational lives. This person, from the time she was a small child through later adult lifetime, was used virtually as a slave. It was ritualistic abuse—what, in China, would be the equivalent of sorcery. Even though her consciousness was that of an exalted being, what was done to her body . . . there was great "temptation," if you will, to renounce all of what she knew at the Soul level to be true of the Light because of the inability to accept what she had chosen to learn from this abuse in that lifetime. The temptation to renounce Creator. The wish to annihilate the Self. The agony of Spirit as well as body that she experienced in this lifetime was very great—the most intense of the lifetimes in which she has chosen to explore this issue.

---

[39] Years later, in a session with Melora, I was to discover that in this French lifetime my mother was a member of the revolutionary underground and that, at age three in that lifetime, I had witnessed her very bloody assassination.

In order to help her, we wish to impart the information . . . her question is "Why?" of course. "Why would one keep coming in and having this happen." "Why in the world would one do this?" "What is the lesson that I'm missing?" are her questions. Her question still, oftentimes, is "Why do people have to suffer?"

The term we are hearing is "refinement of Spirit." This is a potential. In choosing the depth and intensity of this kind of experience, many have been launched on a spiritual path. Many have come to and maintained their vision of themselves as spiritual beings, whereas if things had been "comfortable" they would have been distracted by the physical, 3rd-dimensional comfort and not sought the spiritual refinement that was the intention.

The next question is, "How does this create spiritual refinement?" The spiritual refinement that is created is a result of being so keenly discerning of the finer gradations of things—first physically and then being able to discern fine patterns and distinctions of energetic movement and expression. Oftentimes people come into incarnation as artists to explore this. What our Jyoti has found in lifetimes in which she has been an artist is that this didn't work because she could not create in art what these discernments were . . . the particularities that are part of the Whole, that create the whole tapestry . . . the little red thread over here that is part of the vast tapestry . . . to be able to discern this.

With the intense suffering there were times when she experienced the exquisite beauty of her Soul, and it got her through. Or as a result of the excruciating physical pain, she reached with her consciousness a sweet, beautiful core that otherwise she wouldn't have known existed. It was for that one moment—at which the entire Soul lineage glimpsed and expanded into the awareness of the One—that she made this sacrifice for the good of the Whole. She is saying, "If you are getting this, then I think I'm getting this too." Yet there is still the question: "Why is this the only way?"

That's been the paradigm of the Collective Consciousness of Humanity, played out by the archetype of The Crucifixion.

MELORA: Yes, and so now we are going to work with our Jyoti to release very quickly. We are sending our Jyoti back from now to this time. The being she was in this lifetime is incarcerated in a very cold cell without any comforts. She is shackled to a wall and forced to live like an animal. They just clean her up right before they want to use her. Total abuse. Total deprivation. She [Jyoti now] appears before herself [Jyoti then] as a spirit that, in that *milieu*, she would recognize as a good spirit and as a comforting spirit. She looks into her own eyes in that lifetime as she is shackled like an animal to the wall.

She [Jyoti now] lifts herself [Jyoti then] out of her body in that lifetime to be in that space with her [Jyoti now] where there's no pain—where there is just very loving Creator energy . . . out of her body to release her from that lifetime many years before it actually would have happened back then. We have now changed the timeline. Now we educate her Soul Being Essence about why and where she is now and who she is in the totality of the Collective Being she and Jyoti are part of. We see spirals forming—like DNA spirals—lifting them both up. Releasing the karmic patterns, releasing the separation from Creator, coming to full understanding of the purpose that has served ALL in the collective Soul Lineage.

Now we are "accordianizing" across those timelines and lifetimes, merging them, having the painful, the "negative," karma drop away. Being reinstated is only the consciousness of the One to free all in their work in the One. Now.

A Life in Elizabethan England

In 1979 I first experienced the past life described below when Sharry Edwards hypnotically regressed me in Athens, Ohio. At that time I had seen shades of this lifetime, including a "character" who looked very much like Henry VIII. I was sensing that here was a man who hated himself and who realized that everyone else despised him as well. I sensed that he had scores of illegitimate children, none of whom he had spent money to support. Truly this was a despicable and dark lifetime.

The following excerpt is from one of several sessions in 1994 in which St. Germain "came through" to do physical healing and soul retrieval on myself and on another channel. In these sessions both of us channeled at the same time while we taped what was occurring and what was said. This session represents the beginning of my experience and understanding of higher-dimensional soul retrieval, and it focuses on a past life in which I was beheaded. The session occurred with the other channel's guide, who did tremendous work with both of us while I was learning to channel.

MELORA: St. Germain is working here [for Jyoti] on the upper part of the neck. He is marveling, even with all of his knowledge and wisdom, that the work he did before doesn't seem to be staying done on the physical level.

GUIDE: An Elizabethan lifetime is partly responsible for that.

MELORA: This was a beheading problem?

GUIDE: It was, yes.

MELORA: We say "problem," not in a frivolous manner. It is a deep trauma to all who experience it.

GUIDE: Trauma in the body. Emotional scarring, too, is involved.

MELORA: This is correct, but this [beheading] is, as delicately as we can put it, one of the greater insults of a way to die. To have the head separated from the body is one of the grossest kinds of violence that can be done to the physical body and to the emotional body. Rarely is it possible for that lifetime expression not to be separated from the Core Soul when this occurs.

GUIDE: Are you now receiving more information about how the beheading came about?

MELORA: We are receiving that those who carried out this gruesome process were well aware of the effects on the soul level and that it was more an act of power than of punishment.

GUIDE: It was more like taking her head and putting it on a platter to show some person power and triumph.

MELORA: We are not receiving visual information about that life at this time.

GUIDE: It would be too traumatic for her.

MELORA: We sense it is in the realm of her spiritual pursuits, as they were misinterpreted. Much like the Salem witches—a sense of power in either herbal use or sorcery, or some such telepathic use of power and intuition. Is this your sense? We are not adept at tuning-in in a linear fashion to history [at this time],[40] ask your advice, and would like to learn energetically the process of the linear experience of the energetic equivalent of the life.

GUIDE: All Jyoti needs to know at this time is to read about this sort of activity in the Elizabethan times.

MELORA: The beheading process? We are getting the sense that she was a female in this life.

GUIDE: Um hmm.

MELORA: And she is no more than in her early twenties.

GUIDE: We see she had a "bewitching" effect on this man.

MELORA: And he blamed her for his own lust. But he was in a position of power and this, somehow, was an embarrassing situation for him.

---

[40] This session occurred at the beginning of my work as a channel. Because, through Melora, I can now access people's historic lives more pervasively, it is clear that Melora and I, indeed, learned this process together over "time." This is just one demonstration of the fact that Melora keeps evolving through her work with me.

GUIDE: He did have to prove his vehemence towards this sort of activity in order to stay in power, true?

MELORA: So we are to assume that he was of the nobility. Much like a contemporary politician being embarrassed by an affair.

GUIDE: He proved his "innocence" in the situation by doing this.

MELORA: This is one of Jyoti's major life issues—this sense of being ganged up on, of being betrayed, of being falsely accused.

GUIDE: Being responsible for someone else's misdeeds.

MELORA: She rises up with great heat of emotion when falsely accused. Her third-grade trauma in childhood, in which she was blamed for something she didn't do and then paddled in front of the whole class of children, was mortifying to her . . . feeling that no one believed her. This is a major issue with her: being falsely accused by a person in power.

APPENDIX D

QUESTIONS ON SOUL RETRIEVAL

(excerpts from a group channeling in Boulder, Colorado)

QUESTIONER 1: Melora, since you and I did my soul retrieval, I have had this kind of a "hive mentality." Many of my past lives keep coming up, rearing their little heads in my consciousness. I say, "Oh. That's okay. That's where that came from." Which kind of relates to T's question about where we say, "Okay. That happened in another lifetime." For example, when I start coughing in the middle of the night and I can't see anything, I know that "Pompeii" has come to visit. We haven't had any cigarettes since Pompeii came back to visit. [General laughter]

MELORA: Very good.

QUESTIONER 1: The part I asked back didn't want me to smoke. She said, "You don't need this in your life."

MELORA: When you connect with expressions of yourself in other lifetimes, it's that obvious.

QUESTIONER 1: A hive mentality. I think of myself as "we."

MELORA: Is this the nurse we? *"We* must take *our* medicine."

QUESTIONER 1: I feel more of a hive, as opposed to "we" being my guides. I think of my guides as old brothers and sisters when I hang out with them. But I think of my other selves as kind of a part of me. It's like a royal me.

MELORA: The "royal plural."

QUESTIONER 1: Yes. I'm trying to figure out how to determine "I's" instead of "we's," because I'm feeling that I'm still . . . I want to integrate them further.

MELORA: They feel a bit split off? What tone do you hear when you say "we" to yourself?

QUESTIONER 1: Um, sometimes it's "royal" . . . There's definitely a tone of "I'm here in this body now, so you guys all have to accommodate me."

MELORA: If it is disturbing, then it needs to be resolved. If it is just part of this process of integrating, then apparently it is necessary for a time. A common experience of those of high sensitivity is to believe totally that whatever is going on now—that's it. It's going to go on forever. This is not true.

QUESTIONER 1: Part of my ego is saying, "Well, they're gonna lock you up if they hear you talking to yourself."

MELORA: You might be selective about . . . Just understand that apparently it has arisen out of the process of integration. It is the way that you are dealing with having the soul fragments come back, and so on. Unless they're rebelling openly [laughs], it's probably all right. Just consider that it's something that's going to be here temporarily.

Understand also that the integration process can take some time. Some parts can integrate in a day; others take . . . for example, for our Jyoti there was one soul fragment that took almost a year to integrate.

QUESTIONER 1: Sometimes it's like a big party. It's kind of nice. You're never really alone.

MELORA: As long as you don t get schizoid and dissociate each individual. It might be more diplomatic to relate to these other incarnational consciousnesses more on an equal basis than on the "motherly" level.

QUESTIONER 2: Would soul retrieval be appropriate for my son?

MELORA: Give us a moment. Do we have permission to speak before the group?

QUESTIONER 2: Yes.

MELORA: If it becomes uncomfortable, maybe we should talk about this privately. We are receiving that something jarred him when he was very young—something that happened when you weren't in the room. Much of the sense of "dragging his feet" is because of this. We are not receiving that there are major fragments "out there" but there is this one big thing.

QUESTIONER 2: How young was he?

MELORA: We are seeing . . . between birth and two years old. Something jarred him that he was unable to articulate because of being so young, and it has stayed with him in some sense—but not in consciousness.

QUESTIONER 2: Could it be when we came here to this country?

MELORA: This is more an event, meaning a "visitation." Contact being made with him that scared him. And so he has had difficulty in trusting because of this.

QUESTIONER 2: Thank you.

QUESTIONER 3: I had a question about connecting with other lives. Say, for example, in another life one was beheaded. Is one able to access that other life? At what level is one able to access that other life? Do you, too, affect it in its ascension process?

MELORA: We have expressed it this way: If you picture someone in an Elizabethan life (a female) who is accused of "bewitching" someone, instead of his taking ownership of his own lust, and being beheaded for it, then picture being that woman for a moment. Picture her being in The Tower. It is cold. Experience what you would feel like, knowing that the next morning—or in a week, or whenever—you're going to be beheaded. While you're in that room, you know your death is coming.

Then you're picturing yourself outside, where you're about to be beheaded. You're picturing all the people who are standing there—all the people you love and all the people you fear. And there are people who turned on you, so there are issues of betrayal. And in this dark night of the soul, everything drifts away that is of the typical 3rd-dimensional way of thinking, because you are confronting this moment of truth. All is stripped away but your own core experience of your life at that time.

In that moment it's like a camera lens opening. You have an energetic feeling of something much greater than yourself, and something gives you inspiration. Something helps bring peace to you, even if you believe your God has betrayed you. That something is your future self . . . at the moment your future self turns into you. In that moment, when the shutter opens, in that life there is a consciousness and a bridging and a reunion with a future consciousness or a future expression of yourself. That is how you access a life back and forth across time.

QUESTIONER 3: So it doesn't necessarily play out that you help them change something that they were involved in so much as you work with the attitude, the understanding of the circumstances, as they're playing out?

MELORA: The assistance part usually goes on at night, during dreamtime. Much assistance between incarnational lifetimes goes on then. Our Jyoti's experience is that she has many reunion dreams with people she doesn t know in this life, where she feels her heart is going to burst because this is someone she's missed so much, but they're not people she knows in the current lifetime. When they greet each other there's always tremendous joy.

Whether you remember the dream or not, you do make these kinds of connections with other aspects of yourself. You also make connections with other aspects of those with whom you're involved in this life. For example, a husband, sister, wife, daughter, mother, friends, and so on. You all have relationships with each other in these other incarnational existences as well. So you may not see yourself in that life but you may see friends from this life in that environment, in that particular "historic" period.

It's the same as when you have a dream and you know that it's so-and-so, but it doesn t look anything like them. However, the dream character has their essence. So you say: "You know? This was Matilda," but it doesn't look anything like Matilda." Knowing that energy essence of the person, that "signature" of them that identifies them as that person, you may be tuning in to that signature as it is expressed in another lifetime.

QUESTIONER 4: You were speaking of when you recognize yourself in a past life. You were talking about the window opening. This is a great opportunity, then, to send love and light back to yourself at that time.

MELORA: Yes.

QUESTIONER 4: If that's been holding you in this present, it can give you release and allow you to heal.

MELORA: Yes. Very good. Exactly. So in healing "here," you heal all, back and forward in time.

QUESTIONER 4: And, as you were saying, it's wise to recognize multi-dimensional selves for that purpose?

MELORA: Yes. Precisely. Well-put. Thank you.

QUESTIONER 4: I get this feeling that I'm about to unite with some Pleiadian friends, and I'm looking forward to it.

MELORA: We would say that there are Pleiadians of higher dimensions and lower dimensions as well, and all those doing the higher light work right now are very evident about their wish to be of service to you for your highest good—not merely in service to themselves. Was there a question there?

QUESTIONER 4: Well, it's not so much a question. As we were talking, there was this revelation of certain avenues that I can actually explore out of my great desire for the ascension process.

MELORA: That desire will carry you very far—all this motive force for Ascension to happen for you. When you are clear about that intent, your guides do anything and everything to reach toward you, as you reach toward them, and pull you across. As the honorable St. Germain put it, "We will pull you toward us."

QUESTIONER 4: I give them all permission to do that. [general laughter]

MELORA: There is great joy.

QUESTIONER 1: Am I correct in thinking that people who feel resonant to certain time periods are connecting to their past and future selves . . . people who feel an affinity for a certain star system have beings or entities in their soul hierarchy, that they can call their guides in and ask to access these other entities?

MELORA: Yes, but understand that it's much like ethnic groups, and, you know, America's a melting pot, and so there are many starry influences on people. One young man we know who is very Pleiadian, wishes to have been from Maya [a star in the Pleiades] because of all of the "stuff" with the Mayans, and so forth. We said, "You are not from there. We are so sorry, but you're from another star." As we explained to him, however, he sort of went "abroad" to school, so his sensing of affinity with the star Maya is much as if you spent a lot of time in London, came back to America and were feeling very nostalgic for Great Britain.

In the course of your experiences, and your energetic expressions in other star systems you might consider future, past, or whatever, you have many different "cultural influence" at the soul level, just as you do in this life when you travel, when you have friends from various places in the world or even different parts of the same country. It is the same way in your relationships and your destinations and your "home ports," if you will, among the stars and among your many lives.

When someone asks, "Where am I really from?"—and someone in our last session said, "Well, what if I find out I'm only from New York?" [general laughter]—we answer this by telling you what your most ancient expression as a soul being "was." We would focus on that point of origin. The other aspect of this is your resonance and your signature energy, by which you are recognized and to which those ships out there are broadcasting. They say, "Okay. She's one of us. He's got the Pleiadian signature!" Thus, they're broadcasting to you.

If you picture the sky in 5th Dimension, now, getting literally packed with interdimensional "spectators," you might understand why your jaws ache sometimes. To bring you home, all those light beings are broadcasting their "own" signature vibration to those of that same signature energy information.

Thus, there is also that resonance. For example, our Jyoti has Cherokee blood. She says, "It doesn't show, but I feel it." There is that energetic thing that's even stronger than what you look like. Therefore, you can be a melting pot starry-lineage-wise, but there is going to be a main energy you carry that is your signature. That's what your own family of beings, your home beings, recognize and also the energy that will call to you.

QUESTIONER 5: Is it important to know where you're from?

MELORA: Have you felt a longing? Have you felt that you're not really from here?

QUESTIONER 5: Yes.

MELORA: Then wouldn't that be important? Because when you discover that resonance, that home group, that home star system, and those beings of that system, you find your true family. This agonizing loneliness that so many star children feel (and have felt all their lives) goes away. Your understanding of ascension is now that you are going home. In going home you experience tremendous joy when you meet with them, and suddenly you are around beings of your same resonance and you're home within yourself and with them. The joy of the reunion is shared on their part too, for they have suffered a loneliness for you as well.

QUESTIONER 5: Are you speaking of souls of this dimension?

MELORA: No. We're speaking of beings from your home system, your home vibration. They are friends, whether they have 3rd-dimensional bodies. There are friendships in other dimensions.

Love is expressed, of course, and energetically there are relationships of great intensity. They're what you could think of as harmonizing with another person in friendship, in family, by blood, by marriage, or whatever. These relationships are of a resonance that is only glimpsed here. If you can appreciate that "there" you have total resonance, then you might have a taste of the joy that is in store for you in returning.

QUESTIONER 3: Melora, I would like to know my stellar point of origin.

MELORA: Is it all right to share this with the group?

QUESTIONER 3: Yes.

MELORA: We are receiving Sirian, with a heavy Pleiadian influence. [general laughter] "Heavy" is not a judgmental term. Heavy means that there's a pervasive resonance. There's an influence there that is almost like relationship—almost as if there were a Soul contract, as it were, on higher levels between your Core Soul and another soul. We sensed a sort of double-guide effect that you might be interpreting as conflict when you were younger: "Do this." "No. Do that." "Be this." "No. Be that."

QUESTIONER 3: Yes. I've thought, *Well, if I go the spiritual way, I can't go the material way.* [laughs]

MELORA: This would not be an expression of that sort of thing . . . a sense of guidance shifting back and forth. A perception—

QUESTIONER 3: Two people trying to drive the same car?

MELORA: Something like that.

APPENDIX E

Soul Retrieval Miscellany

Soul Retrieval & Reiki

(excerpts from a session with another channel)

Melora, can we access fragmented soul aspects using distant Reiki at the Master's level with the intent of retrieving them and/or preparing them for integration?

MELORA: Yes. The "how to do it" part has not been answered, but the answer to the "can we" part of the question is: You can *now*. As you may recall, we have hinted in the past that until your own soul integration is complete, both of you in this beautiful synchronicity of *coming together*, as you will [laughs], now indeed can do this for others.

The more stubborn of the encapsulated soul aspects need to be sort of snapped into energetic openness, almost like you would pierce a boil. For others, you could do distant contact and so, as you would ask permission of a *person* from a distance if you couldn't talk to them ahead of time, you would do the distant Reiki symbol and then the Master symbol(s) that *you* will be learning (Jyoti already knows), including the Usui Master Symbol, and you will be calling to those soul aspects and say: "Jyoti asks your permission to rejoin her," or with whomever you're working. Ask permission to rejoin his or her Core Soul, and here is our intent in this process. "Here is what I promise you: When you come back" (and this is the coaxing part that is the equivalent to the shamanic)—saying what the purpose is and how much better it's going to be if the soul fragment comes back. On the Reiki level all of this is the equivalent. In the coaxing part, and where you feel the soul aspect will come back much more easily, it is a sort of courteous thing to do, an enhancing thing to do, and you can do this with the Master-level distant Reiki work. "This is a distant, Master-level Reiki request. Come back, please," and energetically providing, by use of the Reiki ray of energy, the sort of "rocket ship" to bring them back into the body.

When you do soul retrieval using Reiki, you're really communicating with a whole other person and trying to encourage the fragment to come back. So there may be a sandwich technique, where you try the Distant Reiki, and then the soul aspect comes a little closer, as you put it, and then you use the Reiki again, and encourage. Then, with the Reiki, you can do the healing, again in a Distant session, because even though it's not a *physical* distance it's a distance in terms of communicating with energy.

With your sensitivity and experience in using Reiki you will be able to feel energetically if there's a reluctance of the soul aspect to come back, and you have various techniques at your disposal. Remember that the whole process, if you will, can include all of the following: awakening the encapsulated aspect (it's like Sleeping Beauty—it's been lying dormant); encouraging it to come back; providing an understanding that it is returning to a much better situation and environment with love and light; then integrating, and then, with the integrating, doing the healing work.

Using Reiki, you are communicating through the Higher Mind to that part for other people and helping them learn how to do this. It's a very complex process. In addition, if it is their belief and their willingness, say: "Your guides can help you do this; let's work with your guides." Then, in a channeling state, much as we have done with both of you, you can help facilitate, with their guides, a process and actually make that happen faster for them, as is appropriate to the belief structures of the people you're working with, you see.

In understanding all the options by having experienced it yourselves in how this works, and having us explain how this works, you have become authorities on this subject now. In that sense it actually frees *your* guides and their guides to work in the background, as it were, while you speak to the person, the client, on the human level and prepare their minds, their hearts, and their understanding about the process.

We believe that keeping such things mysterious would be inappropriate, that the expansion of consciousness requires the truth—and as much information as the person can comprehend, so they are empowered to understand that they are actively participating in the healing process, which *is* empowerment. This is the critical information we desire to impart—not to say: "Come have a session, and I'll fix you, and I am powerful and mystical and wonderful." We know you understand this. This is why we wanted you to go through this process yourselves first, not only for your own benefit but for our learning process as well, so that in your human experience you could impart this to others (not just suddenly be healed) and then be guided by us. You will understand that you are *participating* in your process in a major way.

We wish for Jyoti to have options in selecting the tools she uses to enhance the processes that she's dealing with, whether it be healing or soul retrieval, or whatever. Do you understand that now all of your soul aspects have come back, and that all of Jyoti's lost soul aspects have returned?

I don't feel that different. I don't feel "blue," in that regard. I feel in a better mood.

MELORA: It is not necessary to feel these emotions anymore. The integration is complete, and what most people experience as having to feel the emotions is the result of another kind of process in which you're telling a story. Therefore, for example, in the shamanic approach there's a journey, and then it becomes very linear. This happens, and then that happens, and then you meet these along the way, and then there's a certain succession. It is the belief structure that says, "*This* must happen before *that* happens, and then this happens and that happens." Although it works very nicely, we're suggesting that, energetically, the integration—

especially with the help of such beings as St. Germain and the highest-level guides—all of the return of memory, integration, healing, can take place *energetically* and needn't be run through the programs of the mind. You needn't track the healing every step of the way with your brain in order for it to take place.

Soul Retrieval, Flower Essences & Other Energies

(*excerpts from a private session*)

The Rev. N.V. said in his letter that Melora had guided him to make a flower essence to assist with soul retrieval. He also said that Melora told him to call down starlight from the brightest star ever created in all the multi-universes. He got the name Ehyeh Metatron Ehyeh.

MELORA: First of all, we did not tell him about the flower essence directly. His connection with what our article in *The Sedona Journal* [*of Emergence*] said triggered a connection with a very high guide of his own—a Native American kind of energy, of which he also is. It triggered him into remembrance, from other lives, of doing this work.

Regarding "the brightest star" of the many universes, this part *is* for our Jyoti. Give us a moment. We interpret this as what has been called "The Great Central Sun." Often those such as the Joshua David Stone group interpret that as being in this universe, as you understand it. We are saying that The Great Central Sun is the core of the many universes.

The Great Central Sun is like a Grand Central Station of communication by means of the light rays of the many universes and the many stars. The number of communication "cables" going through The Great Central Sun are infinite. It is the great central way-station for the communications of the multi-universes. What our Jyoti would be doing in asking for these energies is to be specific in her intent. For her it would not be to create the flower essence; for her it would be more homing in on specific energies to enhance the soul retrieval work on levels higher than she has hitherto been able to imagine. She has gone to the next step in her comprehension of doing soul retrieval.

Using The Great Central Sun energies would be the highest level, meaning the entities' or beings' connections through the many universes of their expressions. *(This is more complex than even we can totally fathom.)*

Because of our commitment to the Soul Retrieval work, our Jyoti is connecting to that which is much, much, much higher in her vertical soul hierarchy in that relay, that combination of relays, and so forth—that Being that can connect directly with her. Of course, this enhances her own process as well. It is necessary in order to bring this through for the alignment of her mental and emotional bodies, which she has been requesting most urgently and intensely right now. When this work is done, the energies flow through her and are grounded into the core of the Earth.

The Rev. N.V. also said that in doing soul retrieval, it would be helpful to bring in Chief Joseph of the Nez Perce, Shannon Psall-Kanum of the Luma and Queen Diagna, leader of this planet's Nature Angels.

Yes. The shamanic approach to soul retrieval has been the most basic used on Earth. Its effects, however, are not as pervasive, as it is not done on the energetic level. [The Rev. N.V.'s] comments are to remind our Jyoti of the importance of using Earth energies in this work as well. In fact, her client in a long session yesterday is working with Aztec shamanic energy and Sioux chief energy. This is to remind our Jyoti that **a lot of this work needs also to be done at the Earth level with the physical body. The effect of shifting, transmuting and cleansing the mental body and emotional body, for example—having those set back into place, so to speak—creates an effect on the physical body.**

Also, bringing in the Queen of the Devic Kingdom is that involutionary, nature part of manifesting change, which creation is. You manifest change. You change from a state in which, energetically, "nothing was there" to a state in which something now appears. The Luma are the evolutionary part, the sort of Great White Brotherhood angle, what you term the "higher spiritual forces." Together, they form a triangle. **You have the shamanic, which is Earth centered, body centered; you have the Devic, which are the forces here to help you materialize into your reality; you have the spiritual part. They form that triangle, and that is that body/spirit/Nature combination.**

Yellow is symbolic of our Jyoti's specific, unique energy signature. In working with the Great Central Sun, as an example, there would be an understanding from the Source that it is she to whom this energy is being sent. This helps it be calibrated at the other end, for exactly what she needs, because her energy signature goes with the intention. Also, her particular signature color goes up into that cylindrical shape, ensuring that the energies coming from The Great Central Sun are interpreted according to vibrations that will reach her without overloading her. The energies will reach her in her understanding, her energetic pattern.

In computer terminology, if your modem is too slow—or if it's set at a different speed than the transmission it's supposed to receive—there are going to be glitches in communication. It is: "What kind of modem do you have? What is your baud rate?"

APPENDIX F

Etheric Implant Removal

(excerpts from a private session)

GG: Something major has happened—a major shift.

MELORA: There was a major impediment to the soul retrieval process, and major impediments in many areas of your life, including your physical health. There was an alien implant of an unusual kind that we have not seen before. What we and our other helpers guided our Jyoti to do was to use the kyanite[41] in a way that she hasn't before. She used all three big pieces and with other very carefully selected stones *outlined* the area of etheric surgery very meticulously.

The implant wasn't a simple pattern; it was basically a butterfly shaped device lodged etherically between the sternum and the top of the abdomen. This has been robbing you of communication, or life force, between your chakras and inhibiting efficient digestion. There has been a problem on all levels—especially in the cleansing organs functioning at full capacity, much problem in the intestines. The connection between your upper and lower chakras was severed so that you were not getting the life force flowing through your body normally.

---

[41] Kyanite is a medium-blue, shiny, striated healing stone.

GG: Where did it come from? Is it a new implant or an old implant that has been there all my life?

MELORA: It has been there for two years. Whatever you were going through in your state of being made your "resistance" be down. Because of your openness to channel and because of your confusion and heartache, and whatever, there was a lowering of the vibration and then certain alien beings took the opportunity to implant you with this. What has made it possible to remove it now has been the other work you've been doing. The constant spiritual work in raising your vibration has actually made the implant rise to the surface, almost like a blood blister. It was actually deeper in your system before but has gradually been "unmasked" so that it could be perceived and worked with by Higher Beings through such a channel as our Jyoti. In a big way, your conscious intentions, desire to receive, more and more clarity— just your will aligned with Spirit to be free of any encumbrances— are what enabled this process to occur today.

GG: I have felt a lack of life force and passion.

MELORA: Yes, and one of the physical benefits will be that you will come more into a healthy body weight and constitution. With the efficient metabolizing and absorption of nutrients and food, there will be less desire to eat certain things like sweets and dairy products that are not of benefit to your body. Dairy products cause mucous to form in the lining of the intestines because of the over-homogenization, antibiotics and pesticides the cows consume in their feed. When mucous builds up in the intestines you can't absorb the nutrients. Your body keeps saying, "I'm hungry," because it's not getting nutrients. Dairy products actually create bloating in the intestines. (If you could get organic, lactose-free dairy products it would be very beneficial.) However, you could tolerate dairy products if you had them, say, only once a week.

With the life force coming back into your meridians there will be a removal of toxins and a replenishing of the cells. As a result you will see a very dramatic shift in your health. Very high, intricate, work was done today. We actually "rushed" you a bit. Oftentimes such intensity of work is too much for people, but it was your guides' decision to take you through this as quickly as possible, including the soul retrieval work that we're about to do. Doing this work at the Summer Solstice really enhances the results, for it is a very heightened magnetic situation.

By having our Jyoti re-weave the etheric web (something we taught her more than a year ago), we have made sure that the implant will not happen again. The re-weaving is not just in the area of "surgery" but re-weaving between the stones that were on all other places on your body: the major chakra areas as well as glands and organ systems. Your etheric web was damaged when the implant occurred. This created leakage of life force and made you vulnerable to astral-plane entities. It is much as when you break a bone. When the cast comes off, the bone is strongest in the place where the break healed. In re-weaving in this manner you are now protected from the invasion of all of your chakras.

GG: What was the intention of those who put in this implant?

MELORA: The alien beings did this to broadcast to you, to control you, to feel power over you, to keep your light quotient as low as possible. However, with those of you who fight it so hard, who resist the lower-level frequencies so intensely, they don't get a whole lot out of it. It would never occur to them, however, to come back and remove the device. It's like when people throw trash out their car windows. They don't go back and pick it up. Even though it hasn't been benefiting them as fully as they'd hoped because of the conscious work you've been doing in the light, they did get their "jollies" out of watching you struggle against their inhibiting of your life force and restricting your healing power. They also enjoyed keeping you in a state of confusion at certain points and just putting a damper on your ability to do a number of things.

GG: It seemed to have affected my meditations as well.

MELORA: Yes, it affected *all* work that you have attempted to do in the light.

GG: Well, I can't express how very grateful I am that you removed the device today.

MELORA: It is our pleasure. This is the work that we wish to do. Our Jyoti is saying, we are "pushing" her to go into many dimensions of the work as she has understood it to this point so that she is *healer* and *teacher*, which are the two primary aspects of her ascension mission. In these ways she can come into full expression and mastery of the healing arts she has experienced in past lives as her soul desires to grow with them to understand now that she needs to go even to higher levels than she can imagine, with our help and guidance.

APPENDIX G

Soul Retrieval Exercises—Present-Life

(from a workshop in Boulder, Colorado)

We are Melora, and we wish to continue bringing you into more of a comfort level in beginning to do what you're terming soul retrieval. We think it's a fairly vague term, but you all have experienced this work with us in some form. We would suggest you not be interested in proving that your information is correct about the other person but, rather, be totally interested in moving your friends or clients through impediments to their consciousness of their wholeness. Their healing may lie in their own process of releasing karmic ties that are no longer useful or beneficial. As long as you're primarily interested in the other person's reconnecting with fragmented parts, which we would wager you all really are, you won't be concerned with your own *performance* in doing this, and, therefore, you won't do any harm.

We are suggesting that you can use some of these techniques just in conversation, just using your own intuitive information—perhaps not at the same depth as soul retrieval sessions we conduct but, nevertheless, beneficial. At whatever level you're working, even the most basic, you can help the person change his or her resonance so that the other fragments are attracted to come back. Thus, the initial work that you do, however innocuous it may seem, actually is very critical because it gets the momentum going so that person can start to call back those other fragments still missing, by the very change of their resonance.

We are going to work with K, for example, and K, if you would, please state an issue if it's not too personal. Everyone in this group is going to work with you and give you impressions. We're going to sort of start the ball rolling here. If you can think of an area in your life in which you feel stuck, that seems to thwart you in major ways in your life, what might that be?

K: Oh, it'd probably be a fear of really expressing freely who I am.

MELORA: Okay. We would like you to work with K one at a time, and we would like to start with J, just because you are used to channeling. You may channel from your Higher Self or your guide. We're going to keep this to two or three minutes, K, based on that issue. Just close your eyes. J, just as *you* right now, maybe not even as your guide, see if pictures come in. For two or three minutes, see whether you just intuitively know something, based on whatever form that information is coming in, and work with what K just said. Perhaps just tell her what impressions you're getting, if that is less formidable.

J: What immediately comes up for me is: I see a small child, this little girl, standing, you know, happy and just playful, and then I see some kind of . . . some presence kind of coming over. And I see her looking up and for the first time experiencing fear and curious as to what that new emotion is.

MELORA: Good. All right. Now someone else, if you would, just kind of pipe in. Out of your own experience and your own childhood, imagine what would have helped you. What sort of situation might you re-create with K? You can take her there, work with that, and help resolve that. You just try it out. If the person is not really relating to it, then just be quiet for a moment and try something else. You may have to try several different approaches.

Could someone now volunteer to discern what psychodrama, if you will, you could help create with K? Take K to that place and time and space, and change her situation there. Change her reaction to that, do you see? Out of your own experience, you will create a scenario to "walk" her through—a scenario that you believe will help her—and see if anything comes up. The first step is the one that J has taken, where she identifies a moment in time when something changed K's happy-go-lucky experience of her reality. The most powerful moment is as things are about to shift. This is where you go to repair what happened. You imagine a scenario that empowers her, that rescues her.

T: I'll take a stab. There's this wonderful little fountain that's right next to you, and out of this fountain comes this beautiful crystalline bubble. It grows bigger and bigger, and it grows between you and this thing that's leaning over you. It's like a protective bubble and so you're within this bubble and no matter what is said or felt, it doesn't come through this bubble because this bubble is complete unconditional love and protects you.

MELORA: Okay. This is for everyone: Remember what we said about taking it one step at a time? T did all the steps *for* her.

T: Oh. Okay.

MELORA: At each step you want to make sure she's with you, and you give her a chance to imagine for herself first. You can give her a little guidance, and then you're also staying open to receiving impressions of where she is, and what she's seeing, so that you can turn corners here, instead of laying out the whole plan for her.

T: Okay. I see.

MELORA: All right. Excellent. K, we thank you for being the guinea pig here (laughter). K, I would like you to imagine standing next to a beautiful fountain. Go ahead, T. You would say "I."

T: Okay. All right. K, I would like you to see yourself standing next to a beautiful fountain.

MELORA: Then you pause, until energetically you are actually able to feel that she's "there." This is very important because in your doing this together, energetically she *is* there. If you just tell her everything, all she's doing is seeing pictures. You want her to *be* there energetically. So you pause, and you can actually feel when that shift takes place. All right. We're feeling that K's still valiantly holding the image of the fountain. [laughter] Now suggest to K that she's going to use all her senses. You're going to ask her questions now, because you're involving her in the process. So you say, "Can you hear the fountain?"

T: Can you hear the fountain?

K: Mm-hm.

MELORA: Is there a lot of water, or is it a little fountain? (See? You're letting her create. All right?)

T: Is there a lot of water, or is it just a trickle?

K: Oh, it's big and grand. And it's round and it's marble.

MELORA: So she's really there.

K: The water's pouring.

MELORA: You want her to become part of this because you want this to be even more and more energetically real. So you might suggest that she stick her toe in there, or put her hand in there. You're going to explore with her and wait. See if the water's warm. Ask her questions: "Is the water warm or is it cold?"

T: Is it warm or is it cold?

K: Oh, it's perfect. I already went in. [laughter]

T: You're already there!
MELORA: In the process of asking questions, if you wait and become receptive, you will receive that she's probably already jumped in—or you'll see it. Then you'll be able to reaffirm for her that you are with her, that it's real.

T: It's wonderful.

MELORA: You see? What happened is that her experience of the fountain already is very different than what you described the first time because this time you let her get into the energy of it. Very good. Let's have D in the same vein continue with this fountain image and see what comes to you. We understand that T's trying to have an intervening pleasant experience or maybe even an energy power or a being of some sort, but K's just enjoying being in the fountain right now, and we don't want to deprive her of that. [laughter]

However, we want to keep remembering the issue, what J brought up, or what we received is the problem: Some dark force, event or person changed this happy-go-lucky situation, probably to the level of trauma or fragmentation. At the same time we're having K be in a space of comfort, we're trying to get to the bottom of what this is. Therefore, we don't want to remove the problem instantly and say, "That's okay. Put a Band-Aid on it. Now you don't have to worry about it."

We have to deal with whatever this is at some point. Thus, the suggestion of the fountain should be in alignment with that goal of resolving whatever this is. You have to keep reminding yourself of the fact that you're working with this issue, do you see?

D: K, can you touch the bottom of the fountain?

K: Mm-hm.

D: Can you walk from one end to the other?

K: Mm-hm.

MELORA: Ask her what she's feeling. Get her sensations, her input.

D: What are the sensations about the water itself?

K: Well, actually, I've been . . . first I ran in circles around and around the fountain and then I jumped in and now I'm swimming around and around the fountain. I've actually sort of turned into a fish. I am having a ball. And I mean I look like a fish, and I'm just swimming like crazy and having a great time, and I've forgotten about the dark figure.

D: What about your clothing? Does your fish have clothing on?

K: *Uh*-uh.

MELORA: D, at this point it's "Well, what do you think this is about? Freedom? Joy?" You're going to start making suggestions about the emotions and the state of being. Are you just feeling tremendously happy, or, ask her! "Just what are you feeling?"

D: But it could stop all this (laughs).

MELORA: Well, no. You don't want to go quite that far. [laughter] Okay. But see now—you don't want her to go into denial. You don't want her just to go into sheer escapism here, which is what's happening. Again, we have to remember we're working with the initial image of a shadow that stopped this. This is going to call upon you to access your intuition and see if you can get any impressions of what might have happened. So, again, you're going to ask her a series of questions. You're going to try to pinpoint what this might be and ask her questions to bring her to consciousness about that.

D (to K): Are you the only fish in this fountain?

K: Uh-*huh*.
D: There are no other fishes around?

K: *Uh*-uh.

D: Would you like other fishes around?

K: Uh-*huh*.

D: Well, if you could imagine another fish—.

K: It'd be a goldfish. It'd have really, really, shiny, fabulous scales. And it would be bigger than me.

MELORA: Okay. So we haven't gotten to the issue yet. We don't want to get too far upstream, as it were. [laughter]

D: Who would feed this fish? Someone's coming to feed the fish now. Who would that be?

K: A dark, grim figure. Okay, so here's the deal. [laughter] I'm in the fountain, I'm swimming around. I'm having a ball. The fountain is really, really tall and at the same time as I'm in the fountain swimming around like the fish I'm also standing outside of it, watching myself swim around. And I'm aware that I'm keeping between myself and a dark shadowy figure on the other side of the fountain, the center part of the fountain. And I'm swimming around. You know the fish doesn't really see it because it's swimming around and it has the outside of the fountain like the wall.

MELORA: Now K's at the point where we can say, "Turn around and look. Tell us what you see." We're not telling her *what* she's experiencing. We're saying, "Turn around. Tell us what you see."

K (coughs).

MELORA: Throat chakra just . . .

K: I just had a little heart palpitation and it worked its way out.

MELORA: Blockage in the throat chakra. What do you see?

K: Oh. It's kind of a Darth Vader-esque-looking sort of [laughs] thing. Caped, hooded . . . no distinguishable features—just dark.

MELORA: All right. Because she's changed this into a character, she's separating herself from it again. We need her to confront it. So we're going to R, perhaps. We're going to try to figure out what in K's reality this might be. Now we're going to let our intuition come into this. We're going to find out if she's still where we were trying to have her be, which is as a child, even though she turned herself into a fish. She's in two places at one time. Part of her is in denial, which is normal, and the other part is trying to protect herself from seeing who this really is.

We still have the protection devices going on: Darth Vader wears a mask you can't see behind. It is critical that we help her become comfortable, that we move her—now this is a critical point—where she's facing whatever this is. We mustn't let her slip out of this moment. So, let's go into her feelings, because the first thing you go out of is your feelings. Since it's Darth Vader, and he's wearing a mask, and the villain is in a costume now, we need to get to the feelings.

R (to K): The person that's standing outside of the fountain—how does this little girl feel around Darth Vader? Do you get a sense of how she feels?

MELORA: Feelings in her body are especially important.

R (to Melora): In her body?

K: Well, first of all, yeah. I'm absolutely feeling fear. But the person who's standing outside the fountain and was previously using the fountain to block the image feels like me at my age. The fish feels like the child me. I've split into those two parts. Anyway, I'm just trying to clarify. What I'm feeling is: I'm not gonna be able to keep the figure from totally spoiling the fish's fun.

MELORA: Okay, so wouldn't this be a perfect time to say, "What do you mean by 'spoiling the fish's fun'?" Do you see? We're trying to get at what happened or what core issue requires you to ask questions to help her uncover this blockage.

R: So how would this Darth Vader figure spoil the fish's fun?

K: Well, I'm just gonna, 'cause I'm assuming that if I were somebody's patient I could just say all this, so I'm going to just cut to the chase and say, well, it's my mom, and (laughs) um—

MELORA: No. You've gone into your mental body. Okay, so you need to recognize when the person is mentalizing. You want to keep her in her child consciousness. We want to come back to the fish from the fish's point of view, not from her adult thinking, mental point of view.

K: All right, then.

MELORA: And so it's—

K: The fish is still swimming. Yahoo!

MELORA: No, the fish is you; the fish is you. So you need to keep reminding her that it's "you" in the fountain, not a third person—not "she" but "you."

K: So I'm in my head outside of the fountain and I've got to get back in the fountain—

MELORA: Back into the fountain as you, as the fish (laughs).

K: As me . . .

MELORA: From there you want her to answer what this Darth Vader character will do to spoil her fun. What shape, what form does that take? What action? You want her to be in her child feelings. Okay. Good. Let's give it another try there, T.

T: (laughs) Oh, you let her off the hook!

MELORA: Come on, T. Come on! [laughter] (To K): We want you to close your eyes and get back into the fish's point of view right now. That will help T because if you come back into your mental thing you're not going to be giving her the intuitive information she needs to proceed with this. So we have to keep you back, make sure you're in that child point of view.

T: As you're swimming around in this beautiful water as the fish, how are you feeling about this darkness outside of the fountain?

K: Well, now I remember that it's there, and so I've slowed way down and am no longer zipping around in circles, having a big old time. I'm still swimming in circles and I'm trying to go ahead and have fun and pretend that nothing's happening, but I can . . . You know, it's like a shadow passing across the sun. I can feel it coming and it's just . . . it feels like it's just a matter of time before I have to deal with it.

MELORA: Now, T. What is coming? What is K afraid is coming?

T: What are you afraid is coming that will spoil your fun?

K: That I'll . . . Well, I'll be told to knock it off and stop acting like a baby and get out and dry off and put my clothes on and be neat and tidy and quiet.

MELORA: Do you think that that really is the whole truth, T? Because we're getting that that's a pat answer.

T: Yeah. That's a surface—
MELORA: Very good. So how do you get deeper than that? Because you know that she's reluctant to talk about this. So, bring her back into the fountain again (laughs), as a fish.

T (to K): You're back in the fountain, and you're moving slowly as the fish.

MELORA: What she's afraid of is what you're trying to get at. What is this shadowy figure, really?

T: What does this shadowy figure represent?

MELORA: Well, no. You don't want to use those *psych* terms.

T (laughs).

MELORA: Back in the fountain! Take her back in the fountain, and now from the point of view of the fish, look at the shadow and now describe what she's fearing is about to happen. Do you see?

T: Okay.

MELORA: So go ahead and ask. (to K): And you be the fish, now! Don't go out of your fish body. Come back into the fountain.

T: Okay. And now you're the fish in the fountain, moving very slowly. And what is it that you're afraid is going to happen?

K: Well, immediately what comes to my mind is that I think I'm going to be killed.

MELORA: There! You got it. Bingo! All right. Now that you've gotten to the bottom of this, we want you to move her out of her association with the fish. Come out of the fountain and be the real child that she was—because this, just as an example, is the necessary link to the reality of her experience, her fears and so on. Otherwise it remains like Walt Disney or something, do you see?
Let's bring her back into the reality of that experience. Now, before we go on, do you understand how much you need to tiptoe, how many times you need to change direction, how alert you need to be to the slightest avoidance and how to bring the person back? The first avoidance is making that third person "her"; you say, "you." All right. She was willing to jump out of there and put her clothes on and leave because she didn't want to deal with it, and yet in order to have this work done you need to have her face whatever it was. So your instincts are there, your intuition, your mind. Yes, your mind, because you're helping create—create, back track, move forward, go sideways and so forth. Most interesting.

All right, let us not leave her hanging. [laughter] D, if you would please, just close your eyes and go into a meditative state. Where we are in this process now, K, is that you are afraid he is going to kill you . . . and we're not going to cue you on this, because we would like you to try to figure out what this might have been about. We are going to try to leave K there, wherever that seems to be. If that doesn't resonate, you're going to try something else, and then something else.

D: So you're afraid he's going to try to kill somebody.

MELORA: "You."

208

D: You.

MELORA: So we have a sense that this might have been a real person? Do you, D? And then you're going to ask her.

D: All right, and I'm supposed to ask her who this might be?

MELORA: No. We're saying to you first, D, as you, do you sense this might have been a real person?

D: Oh, you're asking me. No. I sense that it's a part of her that she's missing at this point, because here's a baby that has no possible foundation of fear.

MELORA: All right. So, what about making "Darth Vader" be less of a hidden entity? Maybe removing the mask and costume, do you see, because you're trying to get to who this really represents. You should avoid saying, "What does this symbolize to you, because you are dealing with a child, right? Remember the child-self? For a child, it *is* or it *isn't*. Symbolism is not really (laughs) the way children experience their reality. It *is*. It just is, right? Or it isn't. Perhaps, as a suggestion, you'll try to nudge her—to unmask Darth Vader and see who's inside.

D (to K): As you see this person, can you take off the mask and take a look?

MELORA: Are you able?

D: Are you able to?

MELORA: You want to give her a choice.

K: Mm-hm.

MELORA: What do you see?

D: What do you see?

MELORA: Go right to what she sees to identify it.

K: A knight. K-N-I-G-H-T (laughs).

MELORA: Mm-hm. No. She's jumped out of it again. She doesn't want to see the person, but she's going to need to see it as a real person. She's just switched costumes on us. [laughter]

K: Clever. [laughter]

MELORA: Good. We're peeling those layers off. Okay. Now, because she's jumped somewhere else, we're going to have to take her back to the point where the truth can be revealed. Again, we return her to the moment where she's facing whoever this is. We keep bringing her back there.

K: So we're back at Darth Vader?

MELORA: You bet! [laughter]

D: We're at the knight's cue. We're back at the knight.

MELORA: No, we're back at Darth Vader. The knight was just a red herring.

R: (whispers) We're at Darth Vader.

K: Good grief.

MELORA: This is where you say: "Can you, or are you able?" If they're not able, you want to bring in help. At that point, it would be appropriate to bring her in now, as she is now, as an adult, to come and help her child-self. Do you see?

D: Could you bring an angel in?

MELORA: You could bring an angel in. You could bring in armies if you want, but you're going to help her. You realize at this point that she is unable to do this as her child-self. So you're going to—

T: Can you ask her who she'd like to bring in?

MELORA: Absolutely. Just say, "Do you feel like you need some help here? You can't do this by yourself?" You keep asking her questions so that she can tell you instead of programming her.

T: All right.

MELORA: Okay. Good. "If you'd like . . ."
K: Yeah.

MELORA: Good.

D: See, I'm tempted to say: "Let's bring in the troops." But how do I go about offering help?

MELORA: You want to say, "Whom do you most trust in all the world?" or "Do you have an angel that you'd like to bring in?" You ask *them* what they want to do because, otherwise, if you suggest something, it may not be real to them because it's not somebody they trust or even know or care about. So again, turn it back to her and say, "Is there someone you would like to come and help you with this?"

D (to K): Is there someone you feel could come and help you with this? Or something?

K: Mm-hm.

D: And that would be . . . ?

K: St. Francis. And Holy Lady Ammal.

D: And how does that feel?

K: Good, but I also want the angelic group I know as Angeluz.

D: Absolutely.

K: And now I feel . . . backed up.

MELORA: Okay. If K hadn't said this, it would be good to say, "Are they all there? Do you see them? Do you feel their presence? Do you feel their strength?" because you're layering and bolstering that confidence and strength. Have her describe them.

D (to K): I'd like to hear you describe St. Francis.

K: Well, St. Francis is at my left shoulder. He's wearing a brown robe, and I talk to St. Francis every day.

MELORA: Didn't he feed and care for birds?

T: Yeah.

MELORA: T talked about the birds, remember?

K: He did do a lot with birds. And he's dressed like you would think a monk would be: in brown with sort of a rope-like thing at his waist. And he smiles the most beautiful beatific smiles, and he's smiling at me. He's very reassuring.

MELORA: How tall is he? (You see, you want her to get into the real energy of his presence.)

K: Not very.

MELORA: Does he have hair? Or is he bald on top?

K: He's bald on top.

MELORA: Okay. (to K) Look at his hands. Are they small?

K: No. They're big. And he's holding his hand out, like a gesture of support.

MELORA: Okay. Let her take his hand, or suggest: "Will he allow you to take his hand?" You want her to connect now with this source of protection—all this, using body feelings and connections just as she would in real life—to connect with her or touch her to make it real.

D (to K): Would you like to take his hand?
K: (crying). Mm-hm.

D: And how about your other hand? Feels so good; feels so wonderful. A long-time friend.

MELORA: All right. Now we want to keep moving with this, and so the others gather.

K: (crying) Yeah.

MELORA: Let's stay for a moment with St. Francis, with this connection with him. (pause) (to K) Can you have him tell you who is behind the mask?

K: He said he can tell me.

MELORA (to K): Do you permit him to tell you? Do you want to know?

K: Yeah. I really do.

MELORA: All right. Have him whisper it in your ear as he holds your hand.

K: I'm trying to think, I'm trying to—

MELORA (to K): Take your time. Come back to your child-self, standing, holding St. Francis' hand, back into your child body. He's kneeling down, isn't he?

K: (crying) He's bending over.

MELORA: Mm-hm. As he kneels down in front of you, feel the texture of his robes in the warm sunlight. The folds of his robes on the sleeves feel very comforting and protective, don't they? Can you see him wipe your tears away with his hand? As a child now, ask him to tell you who is behind the mask. (pause) Is anything happening?

K: Yeah! I'm . . . not getting anybody I ever thought I'd get.

MELORA: Was a name spoken?

K: Walter.

MELORA: Do you know a Walter?

K: Yeah.

MELORA: Given the spirit of St. Francis, what you know of him and his heart and what he is capable of, with his great heart, make a request to him to say something to Walter, to do something with Walter to make Walter disappear from your life forever. Whatever feels appropriate. And if you would, please indicate to us what that is. Ask St. Francis to do this for you, whatever it is. It's more than just protection, isn't it?

K: Mm-hm.

MELORA: Is it within his power to answer your request?

K: He said to me, "I will make Walter go away forever."

MELORA: Wonderful! So, now, watch St. Francis as he does this; watch him as he performs this. And if you would describe what happens. (pause) Isn't there something that Walter needs to give you before St. Francis sends him away? Something to give back to you? Reluctantly? (pause) Do you see it now?

K: I feel it.

MELORA: What do you feel?

K: It's the . . . it's the appropriateness and my right to feel as much joy as I ever want to feel.

MELORA: Yes! Take it back now. Don't hesitate.

K: I've got it.

MELORA: Right into your heart, breathe it in—big, deep breath. Say, "Thank you, Walter."

K: (whispers) Thank you, Walter.

MELORA: Thank you, St. Francis.

K: (whispers) Thank you, St. Francis.

MELORA: . . . and welcome home.

K: (whispers) Welcome home.

MELORA: . . . to that part of you that just came back. Breathe deeply. Now St. Francis is going to complete the request. Would you please describe the manner in which he does this so we can experience his style? Does he have words for Walter first, perhaps? Is he saying something to him, in your behalf?

K: Thank you for the teaching.

MELORA: Where do you suppose is he sending Walter?

K: I have an image of a boat that is going a very long way . . . on an ocean or a huge body of water.

MELORA: See it leave the shore, drift out. It's getting smaller and smaller still. And smaller and smaller, until you can barely see it because it's so small. Finally it is so far away that you can't see it anymore. Please indicate when it disappears from your view. Release it now. Wish Walter well on his journey. Now say goodbye to St. Francis in whatever words (privately) you wish to say to him, and please indicate when you're finished.

K: (pause) Okay.

MELORA: All right. Come back into your body, here in the room. And we say, "Welcome home."

K: Thank you.

MELORA: . . . and we thank you so much for letting us do this work with you. (to the group) Do you see how we wanted to make sure that all the loose ends were tied up? We didn't want to hurry through this. We didn't want to just say, "Okay. We took care of it. Now come back into your body." If you were she, you would want to say good-bye to St. Francis, would you not? We're also bringing her back through the layers that we went through, going the other direction, to the fish and all those other distractions from the real issue. We bring her back slowly and comfortably, as you would in real life.

You saw how moved she was by her contact and communion with St. Francis, which is why we suggested that we just wait and let her feel that, feel that communion with him, because it was so important for her. That's what we meant by staying in the moment and not going mental and thinking, "Well, I *should* do this and I *should* say that" but being really where K is in each moment. In your loving focus and attention to what she's experiencing, keep asking the sorts of questions that enable her to feel, to smell, to hear, to taste, so that it's absolutely real.

The more real it is, the better it works. The more real it is, the more able the person is to go on the journey with you as you keep adapting to the twists and turns that the journey takes. The primary things to keep in mind are what issue she first started talking about or that you first intuitively tuned into. As the person tries to go away from that, you try to keep bringing her back. How many times did we need to bring K back to the fountain as the fish? At some point—and this is something that you'll intuitively know—at some point again, when she's facing "Darth Vader" you know *that* is when you must unmask him in some way. If she can't do this herself we bring in help. Let her tell you the form and shape and personage of that help. Just keep asking questions that will enable her to create that for herself.

Of course this takes practice. We will work with you again this weekend on this because it is our intention that in understanding these processes you can do this in a conscious state, without even channeling, in talking with someone who's troubled—in talking with someone who's at their wit's end or is blocked. You might say something like, "This is going to sound really silly, but I have an idea. Why don't you close your eyes. I just want to do a little guided meditation here," or whatever.

You can use these techniques very beneficially. Closing the eyes automatically shuts off a primary focus of attention for most people, which is their visual perception. There are people who have come to our Jyoti for Reiki treatments and they're staring at the ceiling and their eyes are moving around all the time, and how can they relax? So you say, "Please close your eyes." Then they're not accessing mentally, visually, and so forth.

That's the first step we have suggested. In whatever manner you can weasel your way into having them close their eyes, that would be great. "Just lie down and relax, here. I'd just like to talk to you for awhile," and say what you see. Then, later, you may actually be doing soul retrieval, because this is not something that we wish for only a few special people to be able to do.

This is very critical work for ascension. It is necessary—totally necessary—that this soul retrieval work be done. In understanding these techniques you can look at your own lives and at your own patterns.

You can say, "I just did the Darth Vader-to-knight trick. With myself, as I'm trying to resolve this, all I did was replace one masquerade with another. I go back to the moment where I'm open, back to the moment where I'm facing this, and I start there again, as many times as I need to." We feel this has been very intense, and that we should stop this work for now and ask for questions. We will close down the exercise part of this and then invite your questions about these processes that we've just been practicing.

R: I have a question. So K intuited this picture of herself as a young child with this looming force. If we don't intuitively "get" something, how can we get the person to that place—or to that first contact point?

MELORA: That is a good question. *She* is selecting the moment that she wishes to deal with, whether she realizes this consciously or not. There's more than one possible moment. J picked up on the

Darth Vader character right away, but you might have had just a feeling of discomfort. You could explore that. You might not see it as an image; you might not see it clairvoyantly.

Our Jyoti did not receive clairvoyant impressions for several years. She made a very intense request over and over again to have the clairvoyant abilities come back. However, she gave some restrictions too: She didn't want to see any dark, ugly things "popping out of people." She said, "I want to see only what's helpful for this work. I don't want clairvoyantly to see—you know, slimy things hanging off people," so we honored that.

According to your request, your clear goal-setting, in your spiritual work and in this very situation, you can ask to have that opened up for you in this work. "I want to see more! I want to see these things that J saw or that Jyoti saw." You can intend that. What will happen is that as this opens up (because you're finally stating a clear intention, a clear goal), you'll do a double-take maybe a day later or an hour later. You'll realize that you saw something clairvoyantly but that you weren't aware of it then.

That's usually how it begins, and then that opens up more clairvoyance. Understand, however, that the mechanism for making this happen is your going into a meditative state—not in your trying to guess with your mind what you should or shouldn't be seeing or what they should or shouldn't be doing. You're going into a meditative state and allowing that information to come in. You stay in the NOW every moment, allowing changes, allowing the turning of those corners and so forth.

You might pick up on discomfort somewhere, and you might pick up on a certain age in the person's current lifetime. Jyoti sees "7," "5," "13," and she knows that's a person's age at the time of trauma. This is the most direct way that we can transmit certain information. You may just sense early childhood. You may sense adolescence as a general feeling of whatever adolescence feels like. You'll be able to know from that. You will feel that. Do you see? You can feel that shadow. You can feel that claustrophobic feeling of something blocking or of something oppressing. Do you have any other questions?

T: The fountain was created, but would another way of doing it, then, be that they would come up with an image that would best suit them?

MELORA: That can be—

T: . . . or is it a tool?

MELORA: It's a tool, so your notion of the fountain was correct, and this was validated later by the fish thing that K chose, herself, to explore. But you (to T) jumped way ahead and went really artistic on this (T laughs) and created the help to come in and take care of the problem in one fell swoop. However, this left K totally out of the process! [hearty laughter], so it was not something that could have created any change in her. It was just a lovely vision that would not have taken her to Darth Vader, which she needed to get to, do you see?

T: Right. And so energetically—

MELORA: You jumped ahead. You didn't stay in the NOW.

T: Right. Exactly.

MELORA: You didn't wait. To help her—

T: Yeah. This is definitely a first time for me, and—

MELORA: Of course!

T: I'm sensing . . . it's not fear; it's just wonder at this whole process, Melora, and what I sense is that the more energetically we can both be involved, the greater the healing that can occur.

MELORA: Yes, but the focus must be NOW. So don't jump ahead. Keep bringing yourself back to, "Where is s/he?"

T: Mm-hm. Mm-hm.

MELORA: "Oh, she jumped over here. We need to bring her back here." Remember to go where she is really experiencing it energetically—where her senses are really involved, because it is happening now, and she hasn't budged again.

Bring her back to where we know, where we've experienced that she's definitely "there." Bring her back to that point. We keep leading the person back to whatever point they got stuck—where the person dodged, went somewhere else. We would wager that all of you at the moment when she faced this knew that that was the moment of truth—right there, right? You go, "Ah! There it is," remember? There was a kind of a gasp in the room. There! You have it. You'll know that every time.

The other things we've been teaching here are: What are the techniques, or what are the elements, that are going to help the person complete this process so that the guides can bring the part back? The first step is finding out what this is. The next step is having whatever this person or entity is give her back that part she needs—the part of her that it's been holding and that she hasn't been able to access.

She'll know if there's more than one. Although you may see them, you may also sense them. You may get a number "5," or you may just *know* five, or however many. You need to stay with these crucial elements of that process. Okay? It's like staying with a chronology, staying with the issue, bringing the person back when they go out of their body, when they become someone else or they go into another time zone or whatever they might do to escape the moment of truth.

When you have that, when you're facing it, that is the point of power. That's where you need to be to have this work be completed. You help them You try to suggest things as we did with K:

"You can't do it yourself? Who would you like to bring in to help you? Who is the person you most trust?" You help make this real. Take your time and help them experience that connection as real, like having K feel St. Francis' robes. "Is he tall; is he short? Is he bald? What are his hands like?" As you said, D, "Is he holding anything in his hands?"—anything, so that you come into the total connection and the reality of that experience, as you said, T, energetically. That's correct: both being in the same place and not jumping ahead. Good.

T: If you know that there are five missing parts that need . . . if the person has worked on the two parts, how do you go about getting those other parts back without pushing them too hard?

MELORA: Uh-huh.

T: . . . because you knew exactly when the time was to be confrontational and say, "Okay. This is what you're dealing with now." You know? But I'm curious about that.

MELORA: All right. Again, ask questions. You see, there's something about channeling that people fear in doing this work. In the old days, channels were considered psychics, and so "psychically" they were expected to know the answer to anything if they were good psychics, right? So there's performance anxiety here. "If I ask a client questions, it means I don't know what I'm talking about or that I'm not a very good channel," which is not true at all. We tell people, "We are not a fortune teller. We do not access the astral plane, which we consider a lower plane. We access only the Akashic records—not for fortune telling but for tapping into past lives, for getting that information, and for helping you merge in consciousness with yourself in other lifetimes."

If you take away the necessity of being right in a psychic way or a fortune-telling way, then that removes a lot of anxiety for you. You realize that you're asking questions as a way to help move people forward in this process. It's not that you don't know what you're talking about. You're asking questions that are appropriate to each moment, and people may need you somewhere else, and so you need to ask a question appropriate to that moment or you go on. Again, you lead them back, should they stray away from confronting a real issue that is really going to help them.

If people weren't reluctant to face this, they wouldn't be having this problem and this blockage to begin with. It's something that seems like the worst thing in the world for them to face, and so you try to find (as you would with anyone you love in your life) what the most loving way is. You try to find some options, alternatives or questions that you can ask that will make it easier for this person to face this. We bring in help, and that sort of thing.

We go step-by-step, go back, go over, stay with them, using our love energy to help lead them back. With the fragments, for example, we would suggest you tell people that if they're seeing a specific number of soul fragments they should tell you out loud.

If they work with two fragments and the others are unclear to them, and the other person who originally stole the fragments is holding out his hand and there are five pieces and only two of them have any shape or form, that's fine. You can say, "Do the other fragments have any shape or form, or texture or color?" You can just go for a color, even if there's not a shape. You can just keep asking questions, again, to try to make it as real as possible.

A lot of people just see light. They'll see a sparkly light and they'll say, "Oh, that's beautiful." You then say, "Bring it back. That's a beautiful part of you. Bring it into your heart. See its light spread." You don't just say, "Oh, that's great. Bring it back. Next!" The whole idea is to bring it back home, to "see that light fill you; can you feel that?" Again, coming back in the same way. Don't rush ahead. Again, this is their experience and the more real it is to them the more effective it is. If there are other fragments, and they're really nebulous, that's fine. Just say, "Bring them back with both hands. Bring them into your body." They don't have to see any particular shape.

With one client with whom our Jyoti and we were working, the person just saw a group, and our Jyoti got the impulse in our work with her just to say, "Have 'em all join hands in a circle, and bring 'em all back in!" (laughs) . . . instead of in some linear fashion. You can be imaginative and creative, as long as you're staying with them exactly wherever they are. No two sessions should ever be the same because, in the NOW, they can never be the same. So we really "frown" upon using the same meditation for every single person. You know: Turn on the tape . . . It's not going to work for everybody because it's not in the NOW— every moment. Any other questions?

R: I have one, Melora. So we brought in the fountain . . . was that for a sense of safety or something? What would that aspect do?

MELORA: Well, we were continuing with where T started, so we could show you [lots of laughter and chattering] that T's initial impulse was right on. She just needed to wait to see what K was going to do with it.

D: She put her right in the fountain!

MELORA: And K jumped in and she was the fish, and that shows that she was really into it and that it was appropriate. If she had just been silent or said, "I don't see the fountain," that's your clue that you need to encourage the client to create a scene for herself. At that point she probably would've picked an ocean or a lake or something, because she wanted to be that fish swimming around in it! If it hadn't been this huge fountain, she would probably have created another body of water. So we wish to acknowledge that T got the correct image about where the client needed to be.

D: How do you get the client to that age that K was? "Would you please go back to a younger age?" or something on that order?

MELORA: Not if that's intuitively what you are understanding. What you're getting intuitively is the next step in the NOW.

T: So is the question, then, when you start, maybe in something that J was experiencing: Where do we begin with this person?

D: Yeah. Where do we begin? How do you approach that?

T: . . . and then see what your guidance is from there?

MELORA: Right. For you, in starting out, it's really going to be just paying attention to recurring issues—or an issue—so that you start to see a pattern about what keeps blocking the person. Or you encourage the person to talk about it. Again, you want to avoid worrying about whether the person will think you're just fishing for information, which is everybody's skepticism about psychics: "Oh, she's just fishing. She asked me all these questions so she didn't really psychically get it." You know—if you're worried about that performance aspect, then that's not going to work.

However, if you're really focused on your goal of zeroing in on the fragments or past-life expressions, then you stay in the NOW until you feel confident that that's really what they need to work on. Now sometimes people will give you red herrings, and they'll say this that and the other. At those points you'll keep trying to bring them back to, "What is this main thing that is troubling you and that you're stuck in?" Soul retrieval work usually is required because of being stuck—not being able to move forward, not being all there, not having all the resources at your disposal, which is why you get stuck! Okay. Any more questions?

R: Yes. When will the *week-long* training in soul retrieval be? [laughter]

MELORA: We would hesitate to influence our Jyoti in one way or the other [more laughter], lest we be accused of . . .

R: I was just kidding, Melora, so—only half kidding . . .

MELORA: We would suggest you ask her.

R: I think I will! [laughter]

MELORA: Take the risk of asking her, at this point [laughter]. She tried to give a soul retrieval workshop some years ago and again, nobody came, nobody responded. So . . . she has no confidence that it would be worth the effort on her part. So we'll see. Yes, it was also our intention in Sedona. As it turned out , however, the group composite made it impossible to do this work, but this is initially the way the workshop was structured. We suggested, we asked, to teach people how to do soul retrieval. As you have just experienced, it is no easy, simple process. All right. J?

J: I have a question about K. We sort of left her hanging there in a very uncomfortable place. Then I thought, *Well, remember? She had all these escape mechanisms* [Melora chuckles] so she was able to keep herself feeling comfortable. But the point is, when you're working with somebody you would never leave them hanging like that while you're, you know, discussing . . . *(general agreement)*. And the other thing is, you know, this whole process is just like the process of channeling, and all it is, is an exercise in trusting that your Higher Self is in communication with her Higher Self, and just trust what you get, and take what you get.

MELORA: Yes.

J: And so that's what she did, and that's what I did. So we were asking a question about, you know, how do you start? How do you even get her to her childhood? You just have to trust that you've already made this agreement, at some higher level, that you would be here today, we would be here together, we would be in a safe space, we would create this safe space, and it would be safe for her to heal on this issue that maybe has been going on for lifetimes that she's been trying to resolve. So it's just an exercise in trust, trusting your Higher Self.

MELORA: Yes. And, indeed, this is part of what our Jyoti brought with her to work from—her notes on when she was doing the channeling workshops and so forth, and you are exactly right, J. This is about releasing to, trusting in, a higher source of information that is also you. In some sense you could think of the Higher Self as a future you, just in the way you could think of your present life as a future version of your other lifetimes.

It is through the Higher Self that these communications between lifetimes and between aspects of you—some lost, some not—take place. It is through the Higher Self. So yes. As J said, it is a coming into communication directly with the higher aspect of you, the exalted aspect of you that you term as your Higher self. This, indeed, is what channeling is.

This is why, for example, Dr. Joshua David Stone has written that channeling is one of the greatest accelerators of Ascension that there is—ascension of consciousness. Because the processes you go through (as J so perfectly pointed out) are the processes of connecting directly to your Higher Self. **As you connect more and more with the members of your soul group, with your Higher Self, with your Overbeing, that is what Ascension is: You become conscious of more and more aspects of you that were unavailable to you in consciousness communication before. That is what Ascension is. That is what coming into Oneness-consciousness is. That is what enlightenment is. That is what self-realization is.**

The moment I become conscious that I am one with God, I am Self-realized: capital S. I realize that I *am* God. This goes in stages, and so for the sake of explanation we create hierarchies, names, levels, compartments and so forth. You begin to realize that you are bringing together, as we say, aspects of yourself and consciously: "I now consciously connect with this soul fragment, bring it back and incorporate it consciously. It's no longer separate from me." This is what the experience of oneness is: perceiving no separation, no judgment, no difference.

Judgment says, "You are separate from me; you are different than I am." That separates. Thus, as you come more and more into consciousness of, and union with, your higher aspects, and your other expressions of other lifetimes, so then does your consciousness expand and ascend because it is like the petals of The Flower of Life[42] as we have been discussing. This network keeps increasing and increasing. You become conjoined with more and more of these aspects of you and aspects of others that are also you . . . ultimately in one. All right, thank you, J.

We thank you most heartily for your courage, for listening to our guidance with trust, and especially K, for this process. We hope you feel richly rewarded for allowing the group to work with you as we all learn together these very important techniques and processes. We thank you K (group agreement).

K: Thank you all very much.

---

[42] A profoundly sacred geometrical structure re-discovered through channelings from Drunvalo Melchizedek and used to create one's personal "Ascension vehicle": the merkaba.

APPENDIX H

Soul Retrieval Exercises— Past Life

(from a workshop in Boulder, Colorado—Day 1)

MELORA: There is one facing you from a past life—a male, dark. Are you aware of this presence? He is almost nose-to-nose with you and having an influence on you in your current lifetime.

J: . . . energetically I can feel it. It seems to be a source of some type of anxiety.

MELORA: Kind of a smothering feeling?

J: Mm-hm.

MELORA: All right. Call in your guide to be present with you. Listen internally to what he says, and if you wish to keep this private, you needn't share. However, if you feel like sharing it, that's fine too. (Long silence.)

J: It has to do with an aspect of my being that I had disassociated with (Melora agrees) and had not been accepting of. That is the thing that causes this sense of anxiety that doesn't really have anything to do with me. You know the story or the drama that goes on with that, that was created as a result of that?

MELORA: A splinter personality.

J: Right. So, I guess this is just an opportunity for me to have knowledge of a very powerful presence that I react to with a certain amount of fear and trepidation. It's just a powerful thing for me to own that and acknowledge it.

MELORA: We have heard the term "shadow self"—almost like what they term the darker self? At least in *your* perception.

J: Right. Something that I've judged as being bad. Almost like an overpowering or overbearing kind of energy. So I'm just feeling like . . . Melchizedek is saying to me that it's an opportunity to just forgive that and be accepting of that and let go of my judgment of that, and just let that re-emerge in my being.

MELORA: All right. We would suggest that you ask this in the form of a prayer petition now—a prayer request to have help in this process, and before the end of the weekend this will be resolved. We are being told not to rush in, however, and not to take care of this for you now. We are being asked to wait until we do the one-on-one soul retrieval before the workshop closes. It is necessary for you to ponder this event. We assure you it is not going to haunt you, or cause you undue discomfort, but that part of the process of coming into harmony with this will be between now and the end of the workshop.

Pondering this [and we are not without mercy (laughter) in these processes], the first clue that we got is perhaps to look at this splinter self in the same way that we have described it according to the various filters certain channels have. An Ascended Being will take on certain colors, will take on certain personality traits, and Melchizedek, as expressed through you, is a much softer energy than he might be when coming through another channel.

This is the same as looking at the splinter self so that our first clue was: If you could watch this splinter self transform into the guide that you know, this would be a great help in calibrating or resonating you to that splinter fragment, where you allow it the possibility of being expressed in that way that you know and are so comfortable with. Do you see?

It's like turning a coin over. Any trait has a positive expression of that trait and/or what you judge to be the negative trait, so the ingredients of stubbornness also make you loyal. One is judged as positive and the other is judged as negative. Thus, if you tried to annihilate your own stubbornness, you'd throw the baby out with the bath water, because the loyalty goes as well.

So it is with "the splinter self " It looks to you like the negative side of the coin, but if you turn it, you'll see its true expression to be more like your guide, *and as old issues of fearing abuse of power, also karmic issues of fearing abuse of power*. So there has been a very heightened femininity because the belief structure here is that this will keep that in check. There will be no chance for abuse of power (laughs) when the ultra-femininity is enhanced, do you see? It's only a false perception that if you come into balance with the male, dynamic aspect of yourself you will lose the control that keeps your use of power in check. Does this make sense?

J: Yes. Let me ask you a question, Melora, speaking of this.

MELORA: We believe in striking while the iron is hot (laughs).

J: And let's go to the one earlier, with part of K's question too. When you're actually experiencing this fear or this anxiety in your body, intellectually we know to re-focus our energy on something else and not resist it. The analogy that comes up for me about that is undergoing natural childbirth. I can remember when I was in childbirth telling myself, "You don't have to perceive this pain as pain. You can perceive it as just pressure, and opening," and going through all this technique to try to convince your body that you don't have to perceive this as pain. This thing about fear is the same thing. When you're in process of it, what is the technique you can use to . . . we know to re-focus, but how do you do that when you're actually confronted in the process of that fear?

MELORA: **The pain always comes from resistance—always. And so one needs to be forgiving of the body's resisting feeling the pain.** In a situation such as you described, in childbirth, acknowledging pain as pain first is what we would recommend, rather than jumping to re-focusing. Acknowledge and honor first the reality of the sensation of pain first—then make a choice to reinterpret—but not as a way of blocking, not as a way of going into denial. There is a difference between blocking and denial, and choosing to re-focus as you described, on sensation.

For example, the fastest way to make fear shrink is to stand up to it. The fastest way to make it grow is to give it energy by continuing to be fearful. Facing fear means saying, "I'm really afraid!" instead of feeling the emotion of fear, and then going into denial, or whistling a happy tune. That's a kind of denial. That's a behavior modification that may make you feel less afraid for the moment, but it doesn't actually do anything to change or resolve the *source* of the fear.

Yes, maybe if you change the subject you won't feed it and it won't get bigger, but it doesn't get any smaller either. With anything that you feel repelled by or that you feel anxiety about, actually the more you face it and acknowledge it and say, "You're darned right I'm scared!" (laughs) Or, "You're darned right I'm angry," or whatever it is, the more it shrinks. When you express it, it diminishes. When you block it and deny it, it's held in.

As you know, in some people such denial turns into disease. In other people it turns into mental problems. So with this shadow self, for example, or with setting goals that seem very scary, the desirable thing is to say, "I'm really afraid. This is really scary!" Or "I recognize this shadow self that I've been going into denial about or blocking over actually a long period of time." Is that not so? "And now I'm gonna just take a really good look at it and say, 'You know? I'm really afraid of you, and this is why'."

This is the pondering that we were suggesting you do, J, between now and the last part of the workshop tomorrow—where you look it right in the face and you say, "Here's what I think, and this is why I feel so alienated. This is why I am not interested in talking to you, or why I keep running away from you." State those things, and you will watch the negativity become altered. You will see the shrinking of the enormity of this thing that makes you feel the anxiety, J. Do you understand?

J: Thank you.

(from a workshop in Boulder, Colorado—Day 2)

MELORA: Yes, and we are Melora, and we will save the question-and-answer until later so that we can help J on her path. We will cut to the chase here, J. Is this agreeable to you?

J: Yes, it is.

MELORA: We would like to come to this issue which is at the heart of the image that you saw yesterday and at the heart of what you have been working with regarding T. This is that you allow yourself empowerment only to a certain point, and only where you feel that you are under control with it. You feel more comfortable with your power as expressed in a feminine way. You are coming out of what you would typically determine as feminine energies. We saw very quickly an image of a past life that is very critical in understanding why this is an issue in this lifetime and when you feel it. The image that we got is you as one of those wise crones in another lifetime in which you were accused of being a witch. You were not burned at the stake; you were put on a drowning stool, a dunking stool. Does this resonate with you?

J: Yes, that's my fear of water.

MELORA: Indeed. That would do it. Of course, just as in any other persecution in the name of religion, it was, "Confess this or you die." In the case of witches, it was, "Confess it because you're going to die anyway." The confession was only their notion of saving your mortal soul, which they thought was a fair trade for disposing of you. In the name of God, they believed it was their right to dispose of you. Now here's the thing about the women, especially of your type. There were some very brave women out there who were healers. They knew the medicinal properties of herbs and, of course, people thought this was very powerful.

If someone was dying and you found the herb that would cure them, then this gave you great power. This was a gender issue then, as it still is today. "We mustn't let women have too much power." There are only a few appropriate ways in which you can show your power as a woman . . . still. In this lifetime for you, you felt so centered and so strong and so passionate not only about your right to administer to people who were suffering but also their right to have access to this healing. You see? The strength of that passion made you incautious. You stood up for what you believed in. Isn't this an issue these days and maybe in contrast?

J: (Laughter) Oh, probably. Yes.

MELORA: Why would one be afraid to stand up for oneself and one's beliefs? Even at the cost of your own comfort? Rather than say, "You're really annoying to me. I don't consider you someone I'd like to hang out with, so I bid you farewell." You know who we're talking about. It is your absolute right to be with people with whom you feel resonant. You can do that without accusing yourself of being judgmental. You can simply say, "I do not resonate with that person." There is a neutrality. It's like oil and water. It is a fact. It is reality. It is not a judgment. You can let yourself off the hook there in a very truthful way. We do not resonate. It is as simple as that. All right?

Now let's deal with *this* lifetime. The shadow male energy is a combination of two things: a real person, the one who turned you in as a witch, and a part of yourself that you have estranged from yourself because it reflects that person who turned you in. What we would like to do now is resolve both of these issues—(1) the past-life person who turned you in during that lifetime and (2) who happened to be your husband in this lifetime. Didn't you have to wrench yourself away in an act of expression of freedom, your need for freedom to believe, to practice what you believe? It's the same issue, do you see? However, in the current lifetime, you took your power. You were able to exercise your power.

Let us not throw the baby out with the bath water here. We now will resolve this. Let's go to that lifetime, and your hair was very similar, only you didn't comb it as nicely (with laughter). It was pretty wild. You know: the crone look and the few teeth missing and so forth. This evolved into the archetypal witch. (Add a few moles to make people look really grotesque so that people could justify their hatred.) So you were a wild woman of the fields and the moors, and you still love the outdoors, do you not? You still love that connection with nature. That has not gone away.

We will take you to a point of the most power in resolving this for you and that is the point at which they strap you in the chair, the dunking stool. Now, what we will ask you to do at this moment is to face the shadow person who is your husband, who turned you in out of fear for his own life, who turned you in out of peer pressure, if you will. He turned you in because everyone else needed a scapegoat, and his weakness, his ignorance and his fear caused your death in that lifetime. Don't forget the humiliation of being roped into the chair in front of all of the people who you thought were your friends, in front of your children, in front of relatives, all watching this about to happen.

The fear of being humiliated often keeps people from speaking their truth, does it not? Isn't shame one of the worst feelings one can experience? All right. Do you see his face in the crowd? Are you able to look around and see any familiarity of the faces? Are you able to find your husband in that lifetime? When you look into his eyes, we would ask you to forgive him and send that message from your eyes, as frightened as you are, as betrayed as you feel, as wronged as you feel. Look into his eyes and send him forgiveness. Can you do that?

J: I might be *able* to do it. I don't want to!

MELORA: We will tell you why we are asking you to do this. In forgiving him at this moment, you will transform the rest of his life in that lifetime. You will turn him inward. You will change him. You will save his soul. If you go in anger without forgiving him, he will not learn the lesson in that lifetime. In giving him forgiveness, you go to a death in that lifetime at peace and do not bring that issue forward with you. Do you see?

So there is something very much in it for you to do this. Do this for both of you if you can . . . because it was the death of your body, but here you are today! Splendid and beautiful. So it did not kill you. You're back! Can you bring yourself to forgive him? Bring Melchizedek to stand beside you in this lifetime in whatever form feels comfortable for you . . . in the form of an angel, per-haps, and you can tell us what you're experiencing.

J: I'm experiencing total war (tears) . . . this feeling of self-righteousness. There's this tug of war between this feeling and the feeling of Melchizedek. The love that's there engenders total for-giveness, knowing that he could do that . . .

MELORA: Do you feel comfortable asking Melchizedek to enter your body, in that life that you were (in), in that chair?

J: Yes.

MELORA: Is he there now? Is he inside your body now?

J: Yes.

MELORA: Now, can you have him look through your eyes? Look out at the faces and tell us what you see as he looks out through your eyes to the crowd, including your husband. What feelings come up as <u>he</u> looks out through your eyes and sees these people?

J: I'm feeling warmth and compassion. These people are so backwards.

MELORA: Yes.

J: They are so enmeshed in darkness.

MELORA: Yes.

J: They're just so frightened and I feel so much compassion for their experience.

MELORA: Okay. Are they looking into your eyes as Melchizedek looks out through your eyes? Are they looking into your face, all of them?

J: Some of them.

MELORA: For the ones who are looking into your face as Melchizedek looks out through your eyes, can you have him send them a message of forgiveness and light through your eyes to them? Is he doing that now?

J: Yes.

MELORA: And there's this flicker, this little flicker of recognition in their eyes as they see this. Do their faces change in any way? Are they getting the message?

J: Yes.

MELORA: What about your husband in that life? What is he saying with his eyes?

J: He's asking forgiveness.

MELORA: It's changing him, isn't it? It's so powerfully changing him that he will not be the same. We thank you for doing this because you have saved his soul, not only in this lifetime, but in future lifetimes as well . . . a great gift of love . . . and a great sacrifice in that lifetime. Now we wish you to have Melchizedek take you out of your body so that you're looking down on your body from above in that lifetime. You don't even experience the choking sensations. You don't experience any more of the humiliation. You're rising above with Melchizedek and you see the people from above as they still look at the body that you have left behind.

Are you seeing the light and going into the light? Now see yourself emerge from the light again with Melchizedek, and you are coming closer and closer with him. You're coming back to the workshop, here, and he's with you, and you land softly in the very chair where you're seated. He's immediately at your side. And now we wish to work with the reflection of this experience, the reflection within you, in your DNA encoded like a shadow, the remembrance of your husband in that lifetime. This you've objectified and separated from yourself as a fragment because you did not wish to be reminded of it and because you did not wish to feel that it was a part of you.

Now, as you experienced yesterday, face-to-face, almost nose-to-nose, there is that shadow aspect of you facing you. Are you able to recapture that and be there with that energy? Go back in time, if this helps, to yesterday where you experienced this. Does that help? All right. So Melchizedek is now standing on your right, is that so? Facing you; you're facing each other. We would like you to see Melchizedek pass his hand over the shadow and it ceases to be a shadow. It now turns into a shimmering light. Are you experiencing that? Now have that light come down from above you like liquid if that helps. The shadow starts disappearing from the top and is being replaced by this beautiful, shining, shimmering light. Now see this light turning into sorts of molecules, not just *coating* the shadow, but lighting the shadow up with these particles of light. Now what is your comfort level with this at this point? Does it still feel threatening or alien?

J: It doesn't feel very dark.

MELORA: The energy that used to give it form and substance because of karma is now withdrawn, and so it is not a presence separate from you anymore. It is not merged with you; it simply is not an objectivized, separate aspect that you're guarding against. It's like shadow boxing. We would ask you now to see Melchizedek passing his hand down the front of your body and removing any of the residue of the experience of that lifetime and from this lifetime as you guarded desperately against contact with this shadow. He passes his hand in front of your body, transmuting any energetic residue of this experience.

Melchizedek can also pass his hand down your back if this is necessary. If it feels appropriate he can place his hand on your heart with the intention of healing this. **Understand that the balance between the male and the female selves exists automatically unless a human being objectifies the other half and calls it "my male half" or "my female side," and separates them. Otherwise, unattended, they blend quite easily and nicely . . . and in fact are blended much more in you than you might ever imagine already.** Lack of balance is only an inner energetic disparity that has existed because of what we have been talking with you about—this past life and so forth. The experience with the husband who is the same one as that past life brought it to your attention. You resolved it in certain ways and in certain ways not in this lifetime . . . until now. Are you feeling complete with this now? Please tell us what you are experiencing.

J: I still feel this wave of tightness in my heart. Melchizedek released a lot of it, but it's still there.

MELORA: We're being asked to have the group extend their hands towards you now in this circle of love and see their fingers, their hands and their arms as light hands, light fingers, light arms. With your etheric arms and hands, reach out to J from your group heart and see if you can get any images or sensations of energy block-ages or residues, tar-like residue, or whatever it might be. Just work with that in whatever way seems appropriate for you to transmute it, sever it, surgically remove it, or call in help. Take just a few minutes.

We are asking Melchizedek to assist in this now. J, just sit back and enjoy this and let it happen. There is so much light in your heart right now—like a little star, a sun, with big rays coming out. Very nice. All right. We thank you so much, J, for doing this very difficult work. Now, this is of the greatest benefit to you as you progress on your journey. This has been a major obstacle for many lifetimes since then. It will free you to do even more healing, to do even more empowered communication with yourself, with Mel-chizedek, and with all the others whose lives you touch. We thank you and honor you. We wish you a safe and happy journey home. Our energy goes with you to protect you.

J: Thank you, Melora.

MELORA: It is our very great pleasure to serve you in the Light.

INDEX

CDs & TAPES BY JOANNA NEFF

The Microcosmic Orbit Meditation — Concept from *The Healing Tao System*, by Master Mantak Chia, and chakra tonals arranged by Joanna Neff (Jyoti Alla-An). According to Master Chia, when properly performed, the Microcosmic Orbit Meditation "confers profound and lasting health benefits, strengthening and cleansing the internal organs from within." Accompanying tones perfectly resonate with each chakra and serve as a "sound map," enhancing the visual dimensions of the meditation.

AND

"Meet Your Special Guide of the Light" — Concept & meditation by Joanna Neff (Jyoti Alla-An), assisted by Melora; music by Gregory Davis.

Sound engineering by Gregory Davis, Soul Catcher Publishing (Boulder, Colorado, USA).

The Great Central Sun Meditation, by Melora through Joanna Neff (Jyoti Alla-An). (Taped on 10/25/98 in a Soul Retrieval Workshop in Boulder, Colorado, USA.) According to Melora, "The Great Central Sun is the brightest star of the many universes." This guided meditation takes you on a journey beyond the Earth, beyond the Milky Way Galaxy, to experience the ultra-high-vibrational energies of our spiritual Sun.

Sound engineering by Gregory Davis, Soul Catcher Publishing (Boulder, Colorado, USA)

BOOK COVER CREDITS:

Gregory Davis, Musician/Composer/Graphic Artist:
www.soulcatchermusic.com

"A melody, picture, work of art, or an aroma can trig-
ger a stored memory from that database of time and
suddenly life fills your cup with joy, sadness, happiness, blissfulness, tears . . . but at least you feel *something* and you know you're alive."

Teresa Dunwell, Artist/Painter:
www.angelfire.com/art2/tcc

"I allow spirit to flow in such a way that I intuitively
grasp the energy, vibration and color of many reali-
ties. Images in my work are actually translations of
energy."

Wendy Saunders, Photojournalist:
www.wendysaunders.com

"The feeling is captured by my honest interpretation of
the moment and influenced only from the pressure of
my soul. If you have to think about the moment,
you've just missed it!"

ISBN 141201613-4